SECRETS
of the
CARD SHARPS

GERARD MAJAX

 STERLING PUBLISHING CO., INC.   NEW YORK

OTHER BOOKS OF INTEREST

Acknowledgment

The author, publisher and translator wish to thank Mr. Del Cartier for his valuable assistance in adapting this book for an English-speaking readership.

Translated by E. W. Egan

Contents

Warning No. 1

To the millions of honest players

You often wonder if it is possible to cheat at cards. And how to go about it. It would be awful to think that some of your partners might be cheating, not just for money, but also solely for amusement. How can you tell if a game is honest? I have written this book to show you how.

In the course of my many travels, I have encountered the biggest cheats and studied their methods by trying them out myself to see how they work. As a result I can provide you with a solid grounding in the ways in which card sharps actually operate. Even without trying out these practices yourself or obtaining the special devices used, you will be able to detect dishonest card games, or at least you will be better able to keep on your guard.

However, if you are tired of losing at cards, you can try cheating yourself, thanks to this extremely detailed book, and in that case, you had better read warning No. 2, addressed to card sharps.

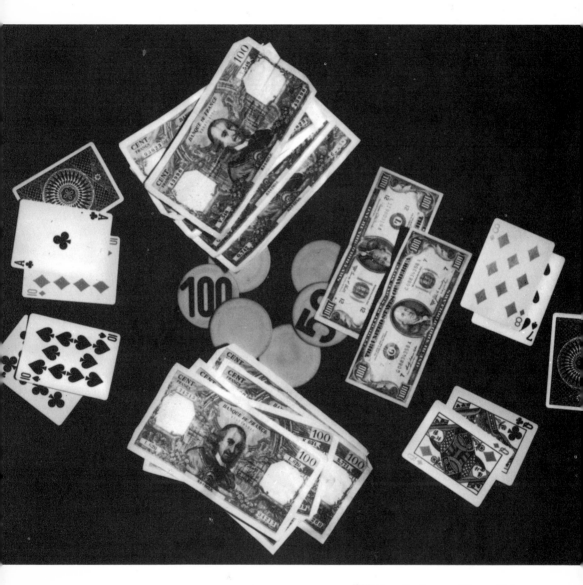

"Wisen up the dupes and there will be
no knaves."

(Robert Houdin)

Warning No. 2

To the few card sharps who are not yet behind bars

An end to unprofessional card sharps! The admirable profession of the card sharp is too fine and too brave to be undermined by a few shoddy practitioners with clumsy hands and poor command of the devices at their disposal, and who furthermore have not attained the psychological level that is absolutely required.

If, on the other hand, you have a high level of proficiency, you are probably one of the handful of specialists who provided me with information on a great many points. I shall keep my promise not to reveal your most amazing moves or tricks, the ones that often are your overweening reason for living. The manipulations and tricks I reveal in this book will make you smile, for they are the ones you do so effortlessly that no one can see them even if tipped off beforehand. You are rich and you continue to fleece your victims even though it causes you perpetual anguish. You're amazing!

GERARD MAJAX

1 **There are so many kinds of card designs that marked cards are not easy to spot.**

1. Marked Cards

People often talk about "marked cards" but they do not know exactly what the term means. Here at last is a systematic study which will enable the reader to establish discreetly whether the cards used in a game are honest. At this point a distinction should be made between marked cards and nicked or cut cards.

Marked cards have a particular sign on the back of the cards, which enables the card sharp to recognize them almost as easily as if they were face up. We shall see that eyesight is not always required and that certain markings can be perceived by the sense of touch alone.

Cards with cut edges are almost imperceptibly nicked or trimmed and it is necessary to understand just how they are used in order to spot them. Marking cards is a matter of vital importance to the card sharp. It enables him to avoid using manipulations or at least to keep them at a minimum. Casinos and card clubs have done everything they can to keep their cards from getting marked.

Marking Cards

First of all you should learn the simplest way to detect marked cards. Just hold the deck in the position shown in Illus. 2 and riffle the cards and, as you do, scrutinize the design on the back of the cards. If parts of the design seem to jump from one card to another somewhat like an animated cartoon, then the pack is marked. A closer look at two or three cards will enable you to figure out the meaning of the changes in the design. We are now going to show you several examples of cards marked by the manufacturer, as distinguished from cards marked on the spot during or before a game.

2 **Ideal position for spotting marked cards.**

3 The clock dial system: the area within the V at A means "Hearts," and the spot at B means "Three."

Cards marked by the printer

These cards must be made and sold in great quantities because the places where they are printed have a prosperous look.

1. The clock dial method. This is a very simple method (Illus. 3). The slender V at A (as opposed to the three thick V's) tells which suit the card belongs to—Hearts. The little white line left out at B reveals the value of the card—Three. Different manufacturers have different versions of the clock and the clues as to suit and value appear in different places. Here are three different cards marked to reveal the Three of Hearts (Illus. 4A) or the Five of Clubs (Illus. 4B).

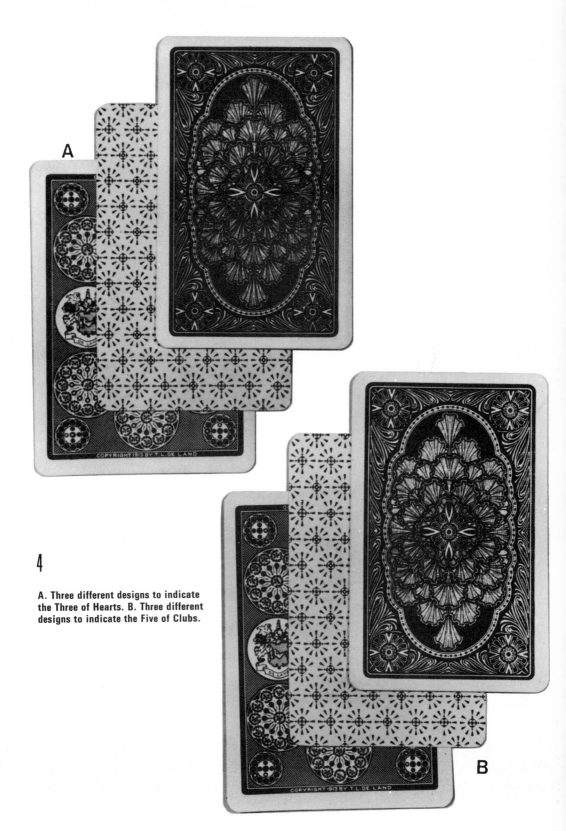

4

A. Three different designs to indicate the Three of Hearts. B. Three different designs to indicate the Five of Clubs.

13

A plaid design reveals the value of the card through different positions of the heavy lines.

2. Plaid pattern : contains wide lines which are nearer to or farther from the left corner, depending on a secret code (Illus. 5): 1 degree of distance = Ace, 2 degrees = King, 3 degrees = Queen, 4 degrees = Jack, etc.

3. The dogs (Illus. 6). The all-white stud on the collar A reveals the suit—Hearts—of card No. 1 and the suit—Clubs—of card No. 2. The white flower petals at B reveal the value, Six for card No. 1 and Eight for card No. 2, if the petal count starts at the top, for instance. The count could start at another point, in which case the values would be different.

4. The landscape. The marking consists of minor changes in the scene contained within the left circle, or medallion (Illus. 7). The feet of the birds are different, and the number of lines forming the horizon varies. On card No. 1, the lower bird has feet hanging from his body—which means Hearts, and there are three short additional lines under the horizon, which means that the card is the Three. On card No. 2, both birds have trailing feet, which means Clubs, and there are three additional lines adjoining the large wheel of the bicycle, which when added to the number of birds—two—gives the value—Five.

6 The all-white boss on the dog's collar at A says "Heart" for card 1 and "Club" for card 2. The flower shows at B that card 1 is a Three, and card 2 is a Five.

7 The landscape in the medallions differs slightly from one card to another. On card 1, the lower bird has trailing feet, which means "Hearts." Three additional strokes under the horizon means "Three." Card 2 says "Five of Clubs."

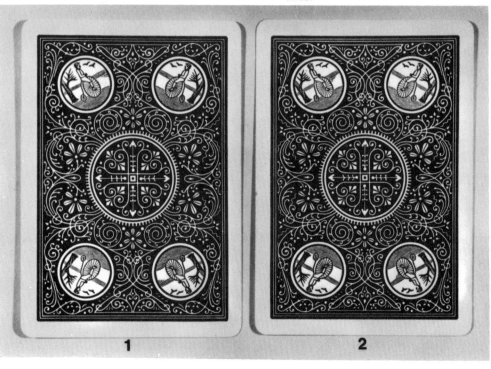

8 The little extra triangle at A says
   "Spades," and that at B says "Seven."

9 Markings on the edge of the card
   reveal the Kings and Aces.

Hand-marked cards
(using inks mentioned in Chapter 2)

1. On a plaid design (Illus. 8). The card turned down is also a
Seven of Spades. The vertical lozenge (A) is tinted—which means
Spades. The seventh lozenge in the top row is also colored, giving
the value—Seven.

2. On the edge of the pack (Illus. 9). The four tick marks nearest the
corner indicate the location of the Aces, the other four mark the
Kings—an arrangement somewhat resembling a thumb-indexed
dictionary.

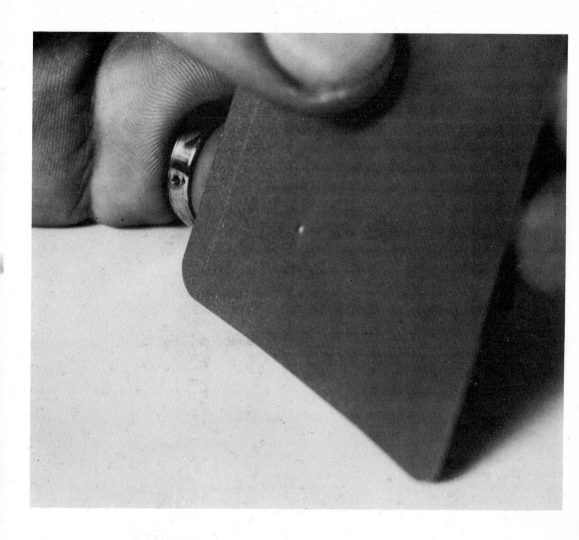

Marking in relief, with the aid of a
trick ring.

3. Relief marks (Illus. 10). To avoid looking at the cards in order to
spot the marks, you can make a tiny dent in the surface of the cards
by pressing them against a very small rounded knob on a special
ring. Each card sharp works out his own code for such dents.

Another simple method is to press a fingernail against the side
of the card, causing a tiny lump to stick up slightly at a point agreed
upon.

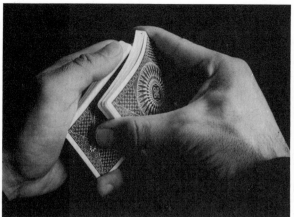

11 Position for crimping one or more cards.

12 Gap formed by crimping shows where to make the cut.

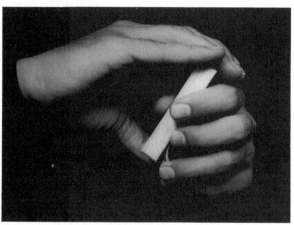

13 Bending a corner.

14 Gap caused by bent corner shows where to make the right cut.

Another technique is to bend, or bridge, a single card or a group of cards so that they curve slightly and do not lie flat. This bridging can be done ahead of time so that certain cards can be detected, but it can also be done during a game. A natural-seeming movement of the hands can conceal the bridging of the rest of the deck (Illus. 11).

An accomplice can easily cut the pack at the slight break caused by the curved card or cards (Illus. 12). The card sharp can even risk letting the "sucker" cut. The chances are heavy that the victim will cut the pack at the desired point.

"Dog-earing" a card consists of folding back, or crimping, one corner very slightly (Illus. 13). This method is harder to detect than bending the entire card, and still allows those in the know to cut the pack easily at the right point (Illus. 14).

4. Aids to hand-marking. The card sharp can mark the cards with the aid of cigarette ashes, dust or even lipstick, if the trickster is female. Some professionals wedge a tiny bit of emery paper under the nail of their middle finger in order to dull the shiny surface of a card at a predetermined point, or to rub off a tiny bit of detail in the design. Once the cards are marked, the bit of emery paper can be put in an ashtray or dropped on the floor.

Nicking and trimming cards

1. The corner : this is done by very slightly trimming the width of an important card, the Joker for example (Illus. 15). All you have to do is riffle the pack with your thumb against the corners until you come to the gap caused by the trimmed card. This method is very useful in setting up a cut that will restore the original order of the cards.

2. Narrow cards (Illus. 16) enable you to cut without fail at the right card or on the first card of a set-up series.

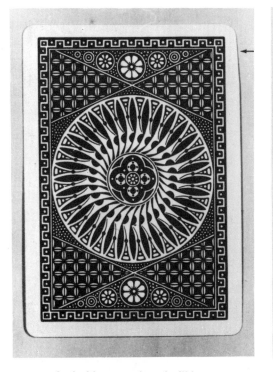

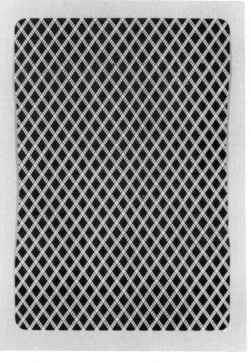

15 Card with corner trimmed will be spotted while riffling.

16 Narrow card guarantees cutting where you want to.

3. *Wide cards* (Illus. 17) are an outstanding means of having another player cut the pack where you want it cut—the chances are excellent that he will cut at the wide card.

4. *Short cards* are used in the same way as narrow cards, except that the pack is felt on the ends and not the sides.

5. *Long cards* have the same uses as wide cards and are used when you know that the player in question cuts by holding the pack by the ends.

6. *Bevelled or trimmed cards* are slightly trapezoidal (wedge-shaped) in shape (Illus. 18), which guarantees that cards, when placed backwards, will stick out very slightly from the rest of the deck and thus facilitate cutting at the desired point. Bevelled cards are also known as stripped cards or "strippers." If a single card or even a group of cards is turned round in the pack, they can easily be "stripped out" of the pack, even though it has been thoroughly shuffled.

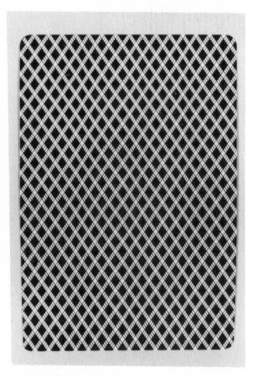

17 Wide card induces honest players to cut at the place the card sharp wants.

18 Trimmed card: the trapezoidal shape is exaggerated to give a better idea of how it works.

19 Device for trimming card during a game.

7. *Trimming device* (Illus. 19) holds the cards locked together so that they can be trimmed with a razor blade enabling doctored cards to be turned out quickly.

Of course a card sharp can use a pair of scissors if it's a question of trimming one or two cards. Some pros take a quick trip to the lavatory to shave off the edges of a few cards against the rim of a mirror. In this way there is no evidence on them in case they are searched.

The scientific cheat is a veritable alchemist who can change cards into gold, at the expense of the honest player.

2. The Alchemy of Cards

The fantastic imagination and inventiveness of the card sharp mixes with the scientific discipline of chemistry. The application of chemistry to playing cards may seem surprising. Yet research laboratories have discovered since the mid-1960's an incredible number of chemical formulas that can be used by the card sharp. We are going to limit ourselves to describing several principles and certain formulas that until now have remained wholly secret and for which the card sharps have paid high prices.

Adhesive Cards

A special liquid applied to both sides of several cards enables them to stick together under very light pressure. Thus you can hide two or three cards under another one, or you can deal double cards. This liquid is invisible and only an experienced individual can perceive it.

Known as roughing fluid, it is obtainable from magic supply houses. You can also make it yourself from the following formulas:

FORMULA A: Mix 100 grams of Canada balsam (a resin used in optics) with 1 litre (1.06 quarts) of carbon tetrachloride (a very dangerous and volatile liquid). Apply with a wad of cotton wool. If the card turns yellowish, reduce the quantity of Canada balsam.

FORMULA B: This calls for an aerosol product (Crystal Clear) to spray the cards, which will deposit a thin layer of plastic on them. This system is perfect for cards that are already plastic coated.

FORMULA C: A mixture of denatured alcohol in which has been dissolved some gum arabic or gum tragacanth.

Tiny bits of wax can be employed as an adhesive—even earwax has been used for this purpose by some card sharps.

The Sticky Thumb

The manoeuvre called the Second Deal (see Chapter 6) will work more easily if you rub your thumb beforehand with a special product sold for use by cashiers and tellers. You will be able to separate cards just as easily as they do paper money (Illus. 21).

21 Product that makes the thumb sticky to facilitate crooked dealing.

22 Device for making cards slippery.

Sliding Cards

If you cover the cards with powdered zinc stearate, they will slide more readily when you want them to separate at a certain point, or when you want to flip them out fast in the Second Deal. You can apply the powder with cotton wool, or better yet with a little device full of powder through which the cards are passed (Illus. 22). A powder for this purpose can be obtained from magic supply houses, under the name of "fanning powder."

Action of Humidity

Some card sharps don't complicate their lives by using adhesives and coatings. They place the unopened pack in a damp room or in a cigar humidor. After a while the Aces and low cards, which have the least amount of printed figures, no longer slide, while the picture cards and other high cards, which are heavily printed, still slide.

Special Inks

To mark the backs of cards you must obtain an ink similar to that used by the printer of the cards. Formulas vary so greatly according to manufacturer and product line, that it is impossible to name a formula that stays the same. They must, however, be marked with a fine nib or mapping pen.

Anyway, since the backs of cards are predominantly blue or red, a quick and often very successful way is to use the ink from a ball-point pen, even if you have to dilute it to the point where it is useable.

Latex Ink

This revolutionary ink disappears when you want it to, simply by rubbing your finger over it. Thus you can disguise an Ace of Clubs as an Ace of Spades beforehand and let another player see it without your appearing to notice. Your other cards in a game of poker are the King, Queen, Jack and Ten of Clubs. The other player will stake a fortune, but by transforming your Ace, you will win with a royal flush.

- Mix distilled water with lampblack
- Add rubber cement gradually, shaking well every time you add a bit
- Apply this ink with the aid of a whittled-down matchstick
- At first, the color of this ink may appear grey to you, but don't worry, it will turn black as it dries
- If your mixture is too thick, you must start over again, this time adding a drop of gum ammoniac to the distilled water.

Varnish for Switching Cards

By mixing equal amounts of colophony (a dark resin obtained by distilling equal amounts of water and turpentine) and carbon tetrachloride you will get a very thick varnish. A medicine dropper

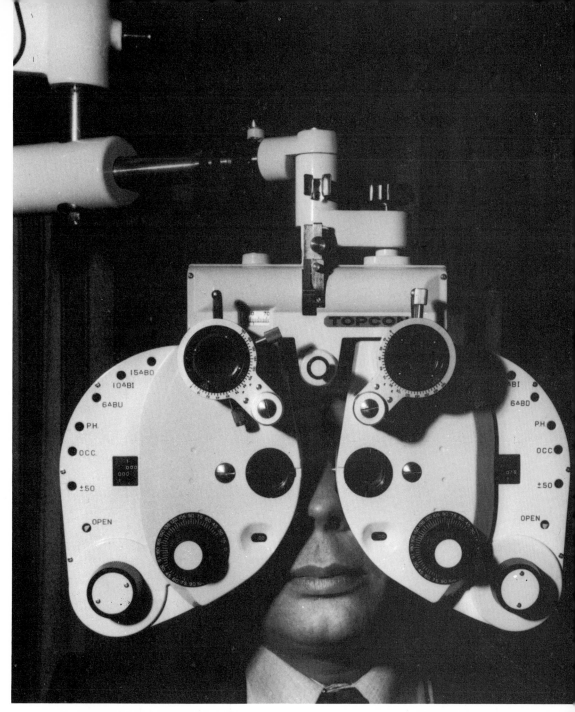

23 **Modern optical science offers the cheat
superhuman possibilities.**

hidden carefully in the hand will enable you to deposit a drop of
varnish on the card table, forming a slight obstacle very useful in
switching cards on the table surface, in manipulations such as the
Mexican Turnover (see Chapter 6).

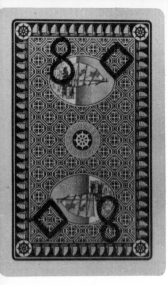

Thanks to special eyeglasses, the cheat can read the cards just as well from the back as from the face. The handwritten inscription is invisible to the other players.

3. The Third Eye of the Card Sharp

Glasses That See Everything

These eyeglasses are part of the folklore of sophisticated card sharps. What exactly are they? Claude Albert, Director of the Centre d'Adaptation Optique et de Contact at Reims, France, has kindly provided some details.

Whether corrective or not, these eyeglasses simply have a red tint that suppresses visual perception of red designs (on the backs of cards). Very faint marks made with a wax crayon in the middle of a red design will stand out clearly since they are of the color complementary to red. It's a very easy way to spot cards while dealing (Illus. 24).

Lenses

Hard contact lenses

This equipment employs the same principle as the preceding but in a much more discreet and unobtrusive manner (Illus. 25). The iris becomes very much darker (Illus. 26). When the card sharp has put in both contact lenses (Illus. 27), people who know him well will immediately see the difference. It is, therefore, in his interest to play with those who are outside his circle of friends. Since all but a few visual defects can be corrected by these lenses, people who are used to wearing these corrective lenses have a decided advantage, for it is not possible for those who are not accustomed to wearing

25 Contact lens with color filter.

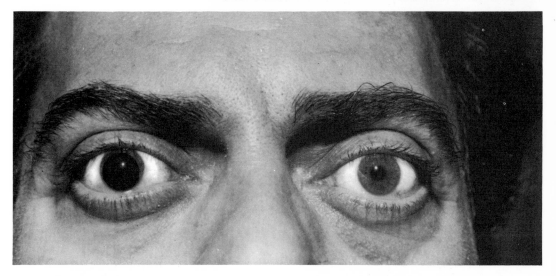

26 The iris covered by a lens appears darker.

27 The appearance of the card sharp is distinctly changed after the contact lenses are put on, especially if he has light eyes.

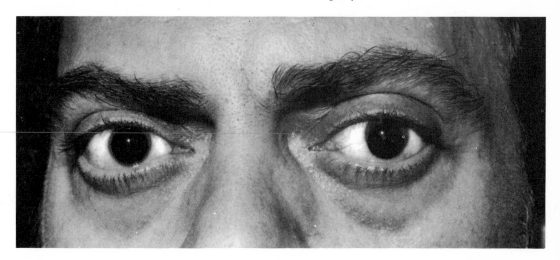

colored lenses to use them convincingly on the day they decide to try them out. Unfortunately, card sharps having a weak cornea or conjunctivitis most of the time won't be able to wear them.

Flexible contact lenses
These new lenses can be worn immediately by even the most sensitive eyes. Depending on the manufacturer, these lenses can be larger than the iris, in which case the red tint will only be found in a circle corresponding exactly to the width of the wearer's iris.

Witch's mirrors or "shiners"

A classic method of the sharper is to use a secret mirror enabling him to see the cards while he's dealing them. The mirror can be an object that would normally be on the table. It can also be concealed in another object that would not arouse suspicion.

Objects that reflect naturally

1. Shiny objects are often found on the table, such as ashtrays, cigarette cases, lighters or pens (Illus. 28).

28 Familiar objects are used as mirrors.

2. If a meal or a sandwich and coffee have just been served, a knife or a small spoon can be used as a mirror.

3. Don't overlook an opponent's eyeglasses, for often his hand can be seen reflected quite legibly in them. Very shiny cuff links can also serve as mirrors.

Special Objects

These objects are manufactured especially for card sharps.

1. A pipe containing a mirror (Illus. 29).

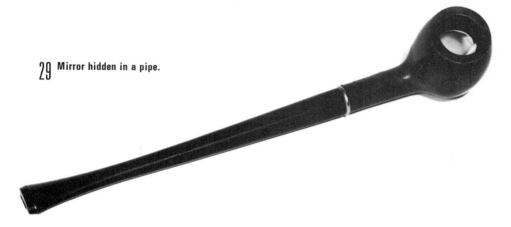

29 Mirror hidden in a pipe.

2. A cigarette with a tiny mirror in the filter, shaped rather like a thumb-tack or drawing-pin (Illus. 30). The cigarette can be held in the right hand while dealing.

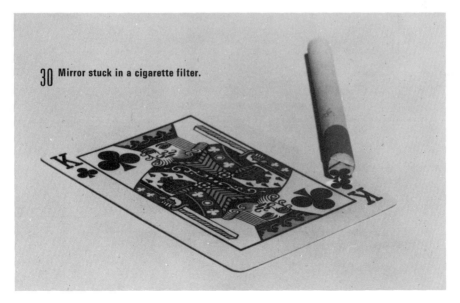

30 Mirror stuck in a cigarette filter.

Mirror pasted to a banknote.

3. A banknote to which has been clipped a small square mirror (Illus. 31). While counting his money, the card sharp can remove the mirror or hide it under another banknote.

4. This mirror is hinged to a ring of metal furnished with a spike (Illus. 32). This is stuck under the edge of the table (a wooden table, of course). You just open out the mirror when you start dealing.

5. This ring opens up (Illus. 33), revealing a very useful little mirror. Naturally, when he finishes dealing, the card sharp closes up the ring, which then looks perfectly normal.

32 Mirror to stick onto the underside of a table.

33 Trick ring, when opened up, reveals a mirror in a good position on the inner side of the fingers.

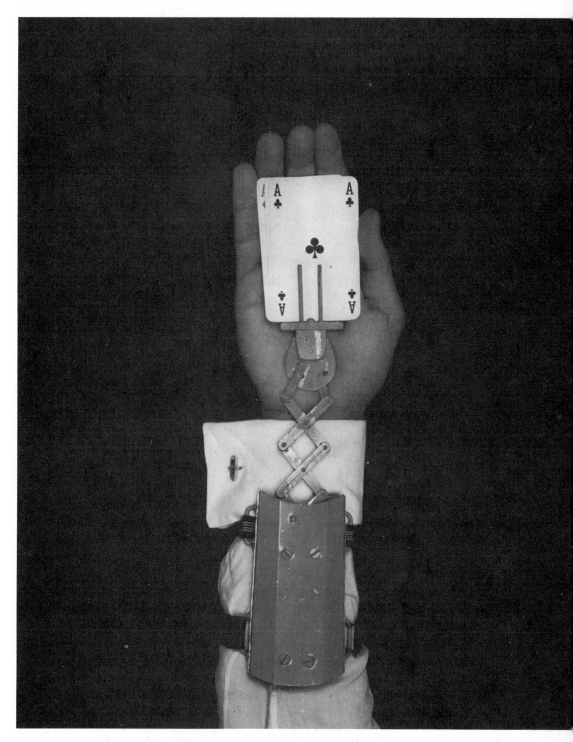

34 This device delivers the desired cards
directly into the card sharp's hand. It
is attached to the forearm by straps.

4. Devilish Instruments

The ingenuity of card sharps has no limits when it comes to creating devices to make their job easier. These devices have always been hand-crafted. However, some of these gadgets have been mass-produced to supply organized groups of card sharps. Furthermore, several states in the U.S. permitted the open sale of these devices several years ago. The laws have been changed and the sale of these things is now illegal. Nonetheless, they can still be found on the black market.

Switching Cards

Emerging unseen from inside the sleeve, these devices, known as "hold-outs," of which some are better than others, enable the card sharp to pick up a marked card and replace it on the table with an undesirable card, in a game of baccarat, for example.

The device in Illus. 35, which is rather old, is attached to the right forearm by straps, and is concealed by the sleeve of the card sharp's jacket. It is manipulated through the cloth of the sleeve by pressing with the left hand on a tiny lever topped by button A in a way to cause an extendable unit (B) to push the card into the right hand. After the cards have been switched, the card that has been replaced is slipped into the extendable unit and the unit is pushed back into the sleeve by the left hand.

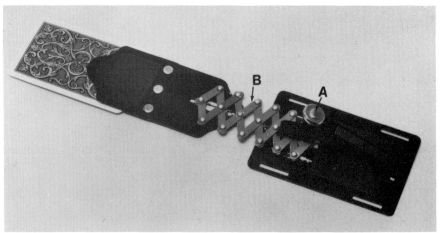

35 A fairly old type of card switcher. Extension of B is achieved by pressing A through the cloth of the sleeve.

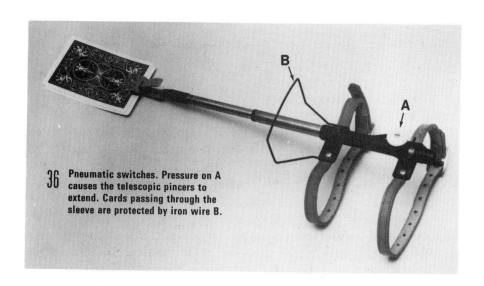

36 Pneumatic switches. Pressure on A causes the telescopic pincers to extend. Cards passing through the sleeve are protected by iron wire B.

This system shown in Illus. 36 is somewhat better worked out, since it is pneumatic and only opens, when the arm is lowered, if the left hand presses knob A. The wire B keeps the sleeve from obstructing the operation of the device.

Illus. 37 shows the most elementary apparatus operated from points outside the right arm. A wire passing through a tiny pulley (A) triggers the unit holding the card, which unfortunately extends out only a very small way. This means that the card sharp is obliged to fasten the device very near the opening of the sleeve. The wire attached to the belt of the card sharp is carried through a small tube (B). Another inconvenience is that the little handle that operates the wire is located under the belt, on the left side of the card sharp.

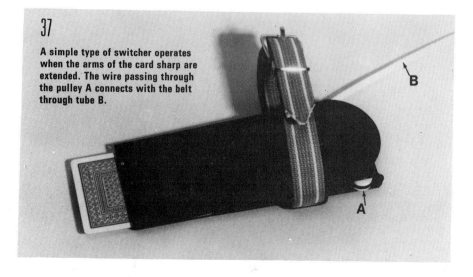

37

A simple type of switcher operates when the arms of the card sharp are extended. The wire passing through the pulley A connects with the belt through tube B.

The system in Illus. 38 is much more modern and practical. The extendable claw provides a firm hold on several cards at once. The control wire is attached to the armhole of the left sleeve by a very ingenious little gadget (Illus. 39). Before the game the card sharp has full freedom of movement, for the wire is long and is held by a bead (A). When he is ready to act, the card sharp places his right hand under the left side of his jacket as if to reach for his wallet. He jerks the wire by holding bead (A). A second metallic bead (B) passes into the device where it is wedged into a spring (C). Now it is enough to extend the right arm slightly to cause the claw holding the cards to extend. When tension on the wire is relaxed, the claw slips quietly back into its hiding-place.

The special aspect of the apparatus in Illus. 40 is that it is operated by the legs. The part holding the extendable claw is attached to the right forearm. The control cable ends in a pulley (C), held by a strap (B) to the right thigh near the knee. The wire comes out through the trouser seam and, before the game, is attached to a

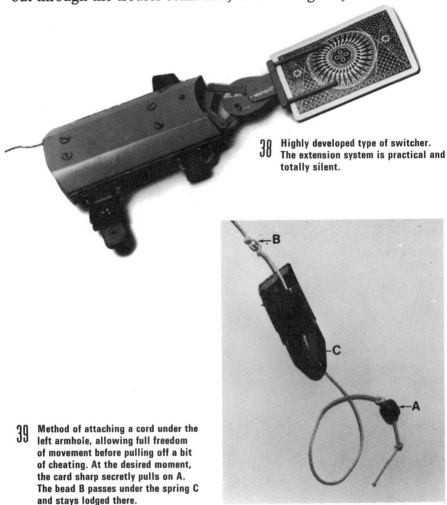

38 Highly developed type of switcher. The extension system is practical and totally silent.

39 Method of attaching a cord under the left armhole, allowing full freedom of movement before pulling off a bit of cheating. At the desired moment, the card sharp secretly pulls on A. The bead B passes under the spring C and stays lodged there.

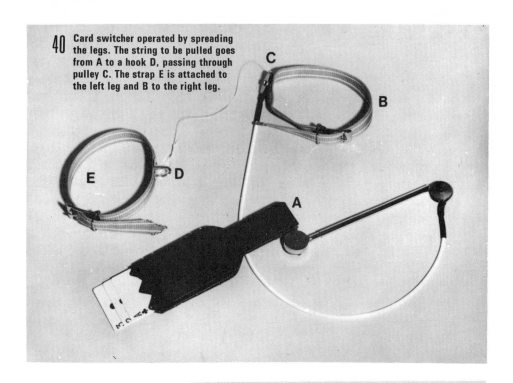

40 Card switcher operated by spreading the legs. The string to be pulled goes from A to a hook D, passing through pulley C. The strap E is attached to the left leg and B to the right leg.

41

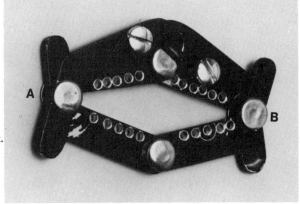

A spring device that enables the card sharp to stick a bead (at the end of the wire through his trousers) simply by pressing A and B to open up the slot.

hook (D) held to the left thigh by a strap (E). The trouser seam has to be open for a length of 2 cm (about an inch). To avoid this, some card sharps use a very ingenious little spring-like gimmick sewn to the inside of the trouser leg (Illus. 41). The wire should have a bead at the end for this. It's enough just to press on A and B to open up the device. The card sharp inserts the bead through the aperture. The spring-like sides close on the bead as he relaxes his pressure. When he spreads his legs slightly, the winning cards are fed into the right hand.

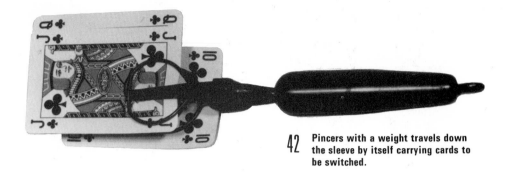

42 Pincers with a weight travels down the sleeve by itself carrying cards to be switched.

This claw with a spring also has a fairly heavy weight (Illus. 42). The card sharp can attach a string to it that enters the right sleeve and ends tied to the left forearm. Extending both arms causes the device to move up the right sleeve.

Ways of Dealing Winning Cards

The devices that do this are for the most part personal creations of the individual card sharp. They provide secret reservoirs of desirable cards. Some of them supply only certain cards, others an entire pack.

The cardboard index file in Illus. 43 holds half a pack arranged in a predetermined order. The tabs at the left correspond to the compartments that hold Clubs, those on the right to the compartments that hold Spades. The index file is kept in the right inside pocket and the desired card is palmed from it by the left hand. An identical index file in the left pocket contains Diamonds and Hearts.

43 Card sorter. Each flap corresponds to compartment holding certain cards.

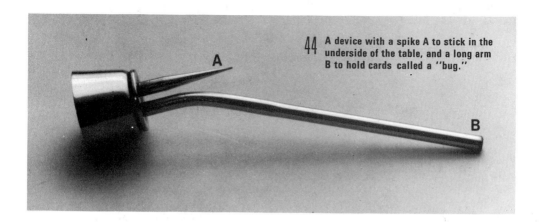

44 A device with a spike A to stick in the underside of the table, and a long arm B to hold cards called a "bug."

The very simple device in Illus. 44, called a "bug," can be stuck into the underside of the table by the spike (A), in such a way that the arm (B) presses firmly against the wood. Before the game, the card sharp can wedge any additional cards he may need, between B and the underside of the table, and introduce them into play as he needs them.

The feeding device in Illus. 45 holds an entire pack. It is attached by two safety pins on side (A) (not visible) to the inside of the card sharp's jacket. Slight pressure on the spring-loaded disc allows the retaining hinged flap to fall open, permitting the stacked pack to be released when the card sharp wants to switch it for the regular pack.

45 Magazine holds an entire pack, and is attached to the lower part of a jacket by a pin (not visible) at A. The pack is released by pressing B.

Important point : A new pack of cards feels cold compared to one that has been in use. The card sharp often has an accomplice whose sole task is to warm the cards by holding them in his hands and rubbing them for a bit, while he discusses some point or other, before putting them into play.

Gimmicked or Gaffed Shoes

The police throughout the world have confiscated "fixed" shoes (card-dispensing devices) when they have arrested dishonest croupiers running baccarat games at various casinos and clubs. Three types of shoe have caught our attention. The first one holds back the first card, at will, letting the second slide out in its place. Another one has a hollow counterweight that can be opened at will to release a planted sequence at the moment when the cards are placed in the dispenser. The last is the most sophisticated, for the extra sequence is contained in the flat metal support. The right hand of the card sharp moves in a normal manner to draw out a card, but the left hand presses on a special screw that automatically releases a card placed there ahead of time. To be quite certain that no one sees this substitution, the card sharp often has an accomplice cover up this manoeuvre by placing some chips or a banknote in such a way as to create an effective screen.

5. Transistors as Accomplices

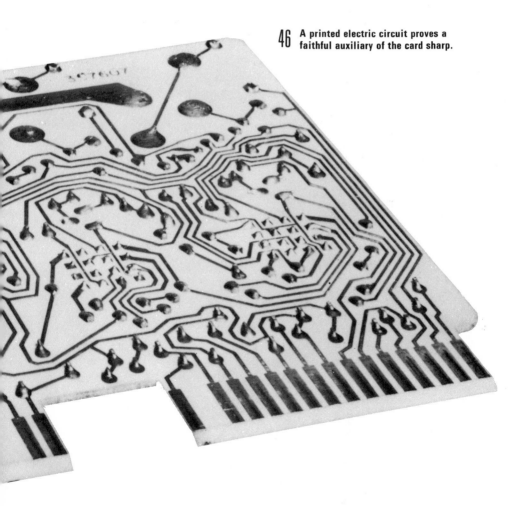

46 A printed electric circuit proves a faithful auxiliary of the card sharp.

For most games, it is in the interest of the card sharp to be in contact with an accomplice, who may be another player or simply a looker-on standing behind the victim. If he can learn an opponent's hand, his tactics can be greatly facilitated in games such as gin rummy, poker, pinochle or belotte (a game similar to pinochle). For other games, such as bridge, where he knows his partner's hand, winning is no problem. We must not forget that above all, the card sharp must be a very good player in order to know how to profit from his secret advantage.

At the beginning of the century, card sharps conveyed information on the cards held by them by means of a form of signalling. This usually consisted of placing the free hand against the face in various positions, such as scratching the forehead or rubbing the nose. A simple and virtually undetectible method employed a black thread attached to the legs of the card sharp at the beginning of the game. A few tugs on the thread conveyed in "Morse Code" information about their hands.

Thanks to transistors, transmitter-receivers can be miniaturized. Although best known for their use in espionage, these receivers are also used by card sharps. We shall now look at some systems of this kind. Transmission is always binary, for only card sharps known to be deaf can justify using a device in the ear, and even then they are still suspect. Another system enables the card sharp to use it by himself. All this is going to seem incredible to you, and yet is not very much compared to the most recent discoveries whose applications to cheating are described in Chapter 11, on the future.

Transmitter-Receiver

The card sharp transmitting (Illus. 47) has a doctored cigarette holder (A) that contains an ultrasonic whistle. The card sharp who is receiving has the following equipment: a special microphone (B) hidden behind a necktie, in a breast-pocket handkerchief or even under his shirt. This microphone is sensitive to high-frequency sounds and triggers the receiver (C) placed in an inside pocket. The latter is connected to a special small relay (D) attached to an arm, in direct contact with the skin, by an elastic band or by straps. We shall show you the inside of this relay (Illus. 48). The small spike (E) has just scratched the arm of the receiving card sharp, exactly according to the whistled instructions from the transmitting card sharp.

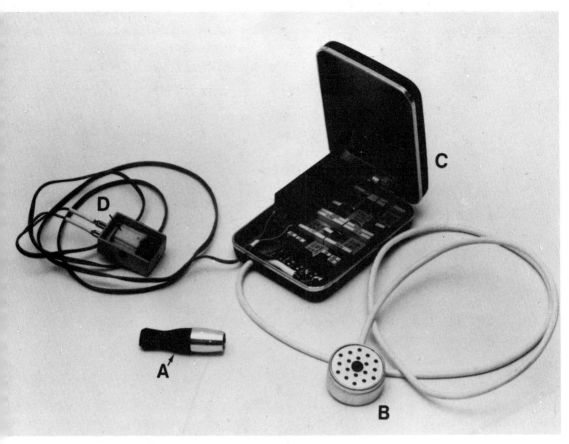

47 Ultrasonic receiver. Transmitter (A)
serves also as a cigarette holder.
Electronic ear (B) leads to receiver (C)
which ends at relay (D).

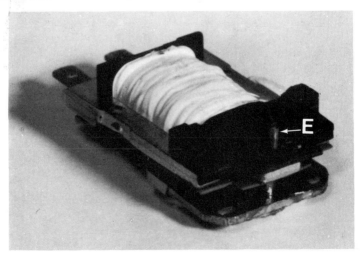

48 The interior of the relay clearly reveals
the little spike that pricks the card
sharp's arm according to a code
previously worked out.

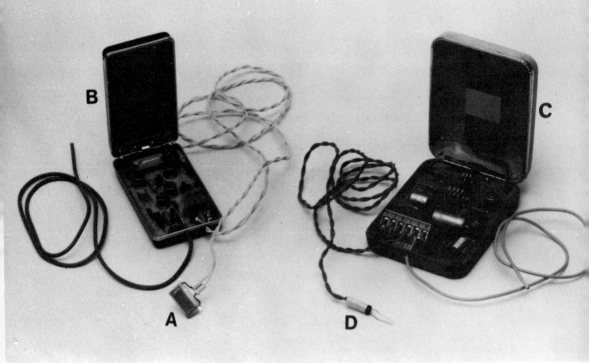

Transmitter (B) is controlled by
contact (A) placed under the toes.
Receiver (C) leads to a little electric
arc (D).

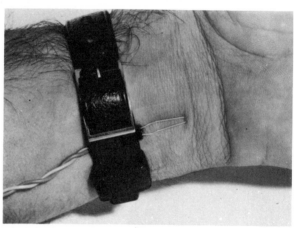

50 The electric arc is placed flat against
the skin. A watch strap can easily
hold it in place.

This system (Illus. 49) is even further perfected. The transmitting
man places the contact (A) into his right shoe, just under his big toe.
Every time he presses on it, he triggers the transmitter (B), placed
in his right trouser pocket, with its antenna running into the left leg
of the trousers. The receiving man has a receiver (C) in the inside
pocket of his jacket. The latter is connected to a small electric arc
(D). The card sharp can fasten this to the skin of his arm with a

rubber band or even stick it under his wristwatch (Illus. 50). Every time the card sharp transmitting lowers his big toe, the man receiving picks up a slight electrical discharge. The frequence and number of the discharges tells what the cards are according to a previously worked-out code.

The Card Reader

This device (Illus. 51) gives the cheat total autonomy. The reader (A) is placed on the right thigh of the cheat just above the knee, and held there by an elastic band. It is placed there at the beginning of the game, screened by the table top; for it to work best the ideal place is the inside of the thigh. In this position it is less noticeable also. It is connected to an electric indicator (B), attached to the left thigh of the cheat. The cheat, who is an amateur electronics expert, has constructed this device along the lines of the photo-electric scanners used at the ticket barriers in the London Underground. Similar devices are used in banks to record account numbers on checks and deposit slips.

The cards he uses are regular ones (Illus. 52) that he pulls apart

51 Automatic reader of playing cards (A) connected to an electric indicator (B).

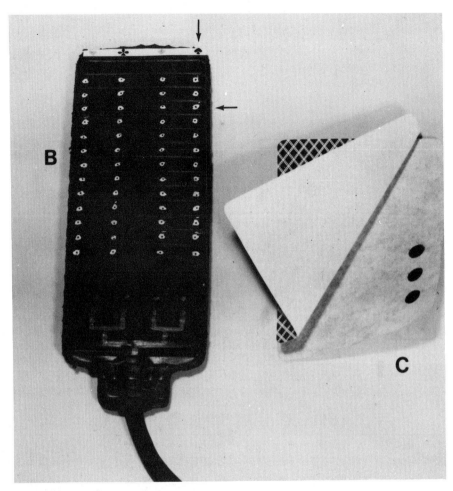

Indicator (B) has tiny arcs which make the skin of the card sharp tingle when he comes to certain cards containing magnetic dots.

(playing cards are constructed of layers of thin cardboard). Then he installs a number of magnetic dots corresponding to the value of the card. These are put in a precisely prescribed place to allow the card to be read. A Three of Spades (C) has been split and treated. It is sufficient to deal the cards slowly while passing vertically over the reader (A). The indicator (B) has little metallic dots invisible in the middle of the white dots. The electric impulse will go to the corresponding column and row, causing a pin to rise. This is detected by placing the left hand flat over the indicator's face and "read" in the manner of Braille. It does not take as long as you may think to locate the card rapidly.

6. Miracles with the Hands

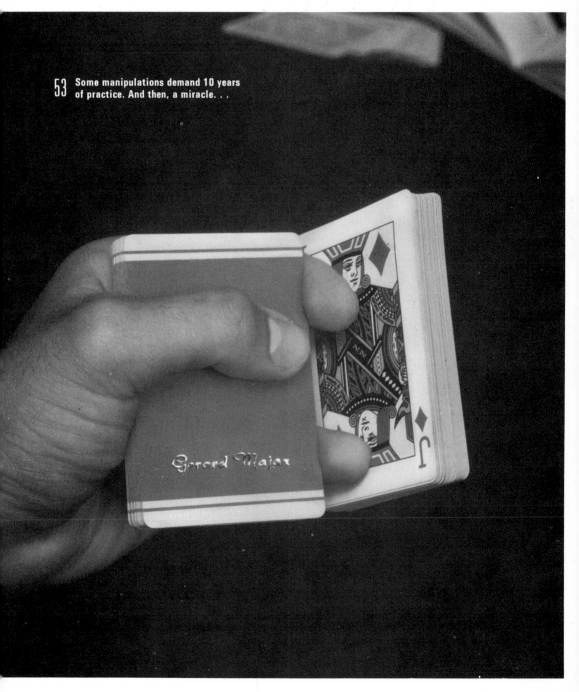

53 Some manipulations demand 10 years of practice. And then, a miracle. . .

While seeking to detect card sharps by noting the abnormal movements that give them away, I have become aware of the enormous difficulty in doing this, due to the infinite number of manipulations in existence. In fact, every card sharp adopts the classic movements, combines them in a new way and often invents moves himself, ones that are better adapted to his own hands. The anatomical characteristics of each aspiring cheat are very important factors in his choice of moves. For this reason, I often demonstrate several manipulations that achieve the same effect, even though I prefer only one of them.

I have above all respected my promise to the very great cheats who have helped me in my work that I would not reveal certain splendid techniques that they are still using. Theirs is a degree of skill attained by only a tiny number of those who attempt it.

These manipulations can be combined infinitely with one another as well as with the trickeries we have already looked at. The explanation of all the principal combinations would take thousands of pages. The most popular ones are described in the chapter entitled "The World's Greatest Cheats." For each manipulation, I content myself with pointing out the most direct application of the manipulation. The purpose is primarily to let you uncover them, rather than to teach card enthusiasts a practical method of making so much per month. If they are truly enthusiasts, they already know too well the value of each manipulation.

False Shuffles

These are shuffles that seem normal but which allow the card sharp to arrange the cards the way he wants, or to preserve the original order.

They are used in most games where the players are allowed to shuffle. Of course, it is the interest of the cheat, when he does the shuffling, to make an accomplice win, so that suspicion will not fall on himself.

American-style or riffle shuffles

FIRST MANIPULATION (Illus. 54)

Cut the upper half of the pack with the left hand and put it to the left of the lower half. The thumbs gradually release the two halves (heaps) in such a way as to let the cards overlap one upon the other. The left thumb has let the cards drop more slowly in such a way as to keep the upper half intact. An experienced card sharp can unfailingly keep the number of cards he wants. A number of repetitions of this movement makes it possible to keep the order of the cards in the upper half of the pack unchanged.

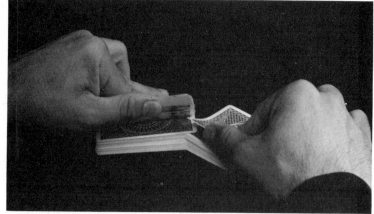

Second Manipulation (Illus. 55)

Cut the upper half of the pack with the right hand and place it to the right of the lower half. The left thumb first lets several cards drop in a block, then both thumbs continue the shuffle in a normal manner. Several repetitions of this manipulation allow one to keep unchanged the order of the cards in the lower half of the pack.

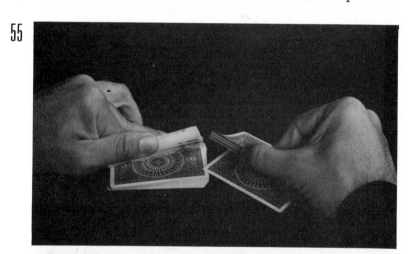

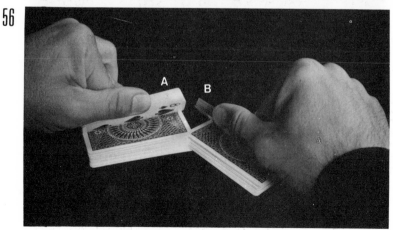

Third Manipulation—The "Push-through"

Cut the upper half of the pack (A) with the left hand and place it to the left of the lower half B (Illus. 56). Overlap and riffle into each other the half-packs with the aid of the thumbs. Move the left hand toward the right hand, while holding half-pack A (Illus. 57). Using the same movement, the left hand releases heap A and grasps the corners of heap B, and the right hand releases heap B and

57

58

grasps the corners of heap A (Illus. 58). Pivot the two half-packs so as to line them up and make it look like an evened-off pack. The fingers of each hand conceal the ends of cards sticking on both sides (Illus. 59).

The right hand draws heap A toward the right, pulls it away from heap B and places it on top of heap B (Illus. 60). The initial order of all the cards has thus been re-established.

61

62

French-style or Overhand shuffles

FIRST MANIPULATION: to gain control of a certain card

Here the shuffle is the classic one where the left hand successively grasps one or more cards with the aid of the thumb. When the card sought (either for its value or because it is the beginning of a series) comes up, in the lefthand cards, you must shift it towards you about 1 cm ($\frac{1}{2}$ inch) (Illus. 61). Continue to shuffle in the normal fashion (Illus. 62). The card will stick out far enough to make it possible to cut at that point.

52

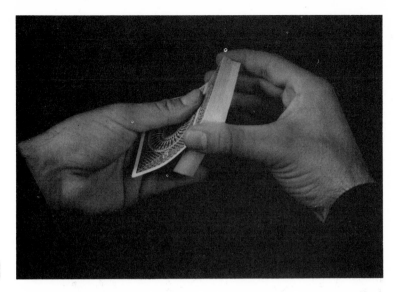

63

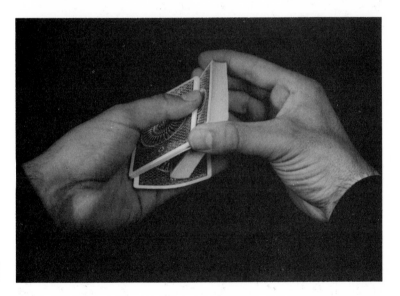

64

SECOND MANIPULATION: keeping control of the top card

The left thumb grasps the first card (Illus. 63), then grasps a small group of cards, which fall on the first card (Illus. 64). You must continue in the same fashion for the rest of the pack. The top card will then be passed under the pack and become the bottom card. If you wish to bring it back to the top, simply begin to shuffle again letting the cards come off one by one.

THIRD MANIPULATION: Top and Bottom, Under and Over, or the Haymaker's Shuffle

The left hand grasps two cards simultaneously. The upper one with the thumb, and the lower one, with the middle finger secretly (Illus. 65). This shuffle makes it very easy to get the pack ready for some trickery. For example, take five Spades—the Ten, Jack, Queen, King and Ace and place them under the pack.

Effecting the "top and bottom" manoeuvre described above leaves the top and bottom cards together in the left hand. With the left thumb, slide off three cards from the top of the pack onto these.

65

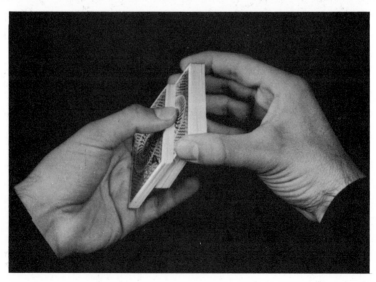

66

Do this again four times and place the whole stack in the left hand on top of the pack. The set-up is now ready. Continue with a false shuffle, which retains the stack intact on the top part of the pack. Deal five hands of poker. You will get a royal flush.

FOURTH MANIPULATION: Shuffle to leave the pack in its original order

The left hand grasps about 1/3 of the pack (A) with the aid of the thumb (Illus. 66). The rest of the pack is put on top of A (Illus. 67). The right hand secretly grips A (Illus. 68). The left thumb grasps part of B, representing a further third of the pack, while the right hand lifts the remainder of B plus A (Illus. 69). The right hand comes

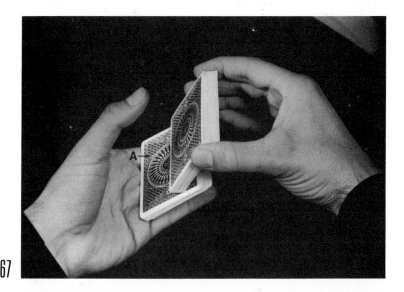

67

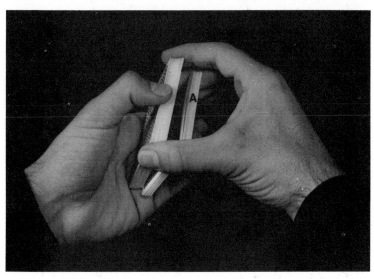

68

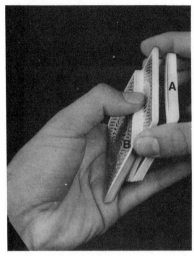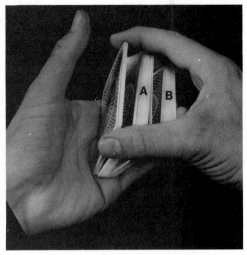

on top of B in order to place A there (Illus. 70). The right hand no longer holds the rest of the pack and places it under AB (Illus. 71). This movement must be done so rapidly that the illusion of a normal shuffle is created. In actual fact, however, the original order of the pack remains wholly undisturbed.

Perfect Shuffle, also called Butt or Faro Shuffle

Also known as the "weave shuffle," this shuffle is called "perfect" because the cards overlap one another very exactly and because it requires a great deal of skill. You must cut the pack in the middle and place the two halves end to end and push slightly. Although this requires a great deal of practice, after a great many tries you will be surprised to see the cards fit in themselves, one upon the other (Illus. 72). Card sharps often make this manipulation without picking up the cards from the table (Illus. 73).

This "perfect" shuffle has some astonishing mathematical particularities. For example, a card in 6th place is going to pass to the 12th place in what is called an "inside" shuffle (the first card coming after the second) and to 24th place after two shuffles, and so on. You have to know that eight perfect shuffles restore the original order of the cards. You only have to see that the top card is always the card that was on top of the pack first (this shuffle is called an "outside" one).

The simplest application for poker consists in placing the four Aces on top of the pack. Then do two inside shuffles. A four-way deal will automatically give you the four Aces.

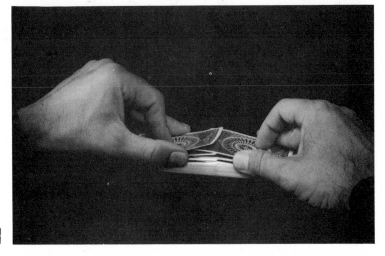

Detection

Those likely to be cheating:

- Players who are too precise in the way they place their cards in relation to one another.
- Players who are not happy to have you shuffle after they have.
- Players who break the rhythm of their shuffle.
- Shuffles that end with an unnecessary cut.
- Shuffles that end in too sloppy fashion, with the hands covering the cards more than would be normal.

False Cutting

This is a question of nullifying the cut made by another player. Thus the cheat who shuffled can without fear ask for this cut. The order of the stacked deck will be maintained. Once he has picked up the cards after the cut, all he has to do is reverse the cut either with one hand or with two. There has to be a sufficient distraction of the other players' attention in order to camouflage this movement.

FIRST MANIPULATION: One-Hand Shift

The pack is cut into two piles and the heaps (half-packs) are picked up with the right hand. They are placed one on top of the other in the left hand (heap B on the bottom, heap A on top). A gap between them is maintained by having the thumb hold the top heap from above, with the other fingers gripping in a block the lower heap (Illus. 74). The index and little fingers are bent to squeeze heap B (Illus. 75). The thumb spreads out from heap A. The other

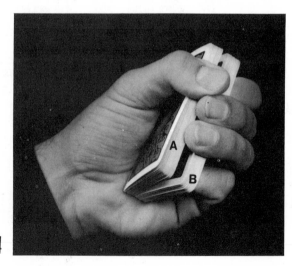

74

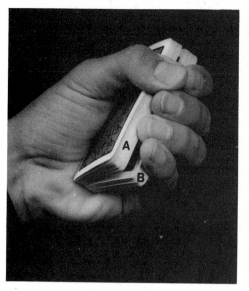

75

76

fingers unbend while still holding heap B (Illus. 76). The thumb shoves heap A toward the palm of the hand (Illus. 77). The fingers reclose in such a way as to place B on A. The thumb withdraws and then comes back to rest on the whole pack (Illus. 78). The index and little fingers have only to pull away from the middle of the pack to manage to hold it normally on top.

77

78

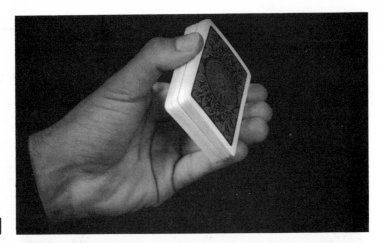

79

80

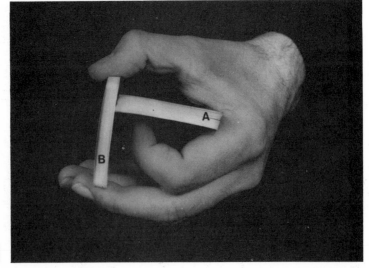

81

82

Second Manipulation: One-Hand Shift

After picking up the two heaps in a normal manner, hold the pack in the left hand, between the tip of the thumb and the tips of the other fingers (Illus. 79). A narrow card or a wide one or one that is nicked or crimped allows the thumb to separate the pack again. You must release the lower heap A, and let it drop into your palm. Heap B remains in the air (Illus. 80). The index finger raises the side of heap A and pivots it (Illus. 81). The manipulation continues until heap B can drop against the palm (Illus. 82). The index finger pulls back to allow B to be lowered completely. The thumb holds A lightly before placing it on B (Illus. 83).

83

THIRD MANIPULATION: Two Hand Shift

The two heaps are picked up one after the other by the card sharp and placed in the left hand. Heap A on bottom, heap B on top (Illus. 84). The left little finger is placed between both heaps, an action somewhat shielded by the right hand from the other players (Illus. 85). The right hand holds heap A firmly between the thumb and fingertips. The fingers of the left hand unbend, which makes heap B pivot, concealed by the right hand (Illus. 86). The right hand raises heap A, making it pivot (Illus. 87). The fingers of the left hand close in order to bring heap B into the palm (Illus. 88). The right hand has only to put heap A on heap B.

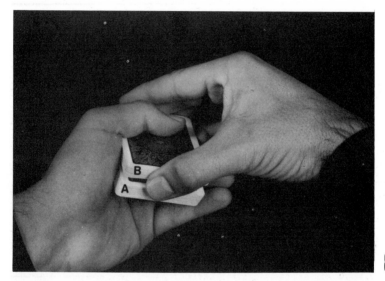

84

85

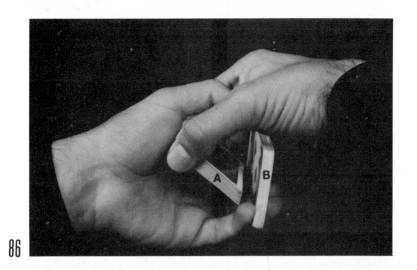

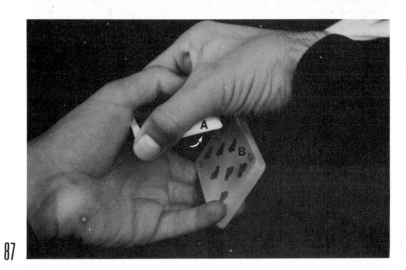

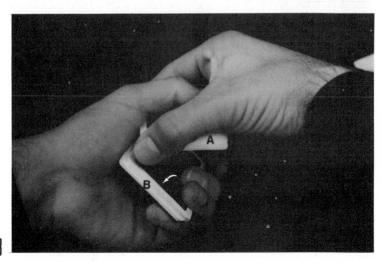

FOURTH MANIPULATION: Shift with One Hand on the Table

This shift is no doubt the most effective. The right hand grasps heap B and puts it on heap A, while effecting a cut (Illus. 89). The right hand raises the two heaps while carrying out the following manipulation: the thumb and index finger continue to hold heap B while the three other fingers (middle, ring and little) close in order

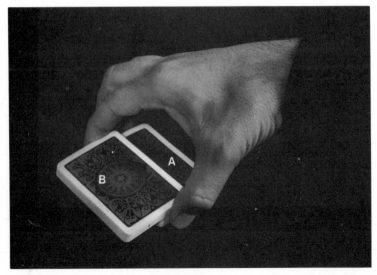

to regrip heap A by themselves (Illus. 90). These fingers raise heap A while the thumb and index relax in order to lower heap B and slide it under heap A (Illus. 91). The left hand then moves toward the right hand under the pretext of straightening the pack and pushes heap B until it lies squarely under heap A (Illus. 92).

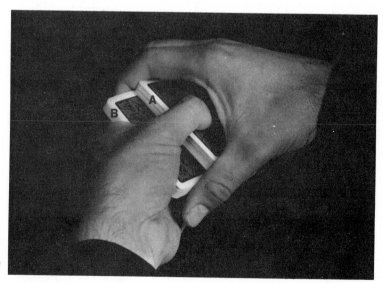

93

FIFTH MANIPULATION: The Crazy Shift

This is called the Crazy Shift because it happens by itself. No special manipulation. You must simply count on the inattention of the other players and pull it off in a very natural-appearing way. Instead of picking up heap A in the usual way, your right hand must move toward heap B and grab it (Illus. 93). The right hand has just placed heap B in the left hand (Illus. 94). The right hand next goes and grabs heap A and places it smack on top of heap B (Illus. 95). You must execute this movement in a mechanical way. If a player notices the inversion, it can always pass for clumsiness.

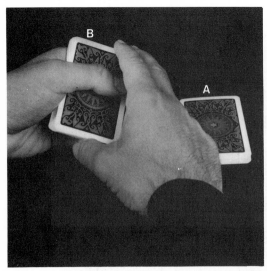

94

95

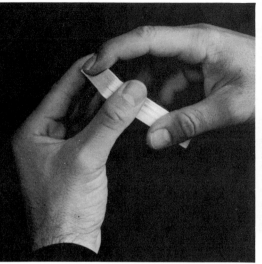
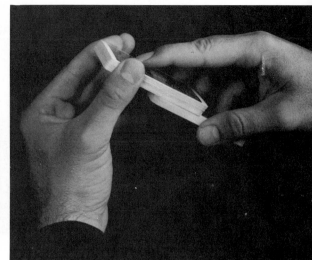

SIXTH MANIPULATION: The False Cut

This variation allows the card sharp to give the illusion of cutting. The pack is held in the left hand. The right hand moves over the left with the index finger poised as though about to make the cut (Illus. 96). The right hand moves away abruptly, grasping a heap off the bottom, while letting the index finger slide over the top of the pack (Illus. 97). If the movement is rapid enough, the players should have the impression that a heap from the top has just been picked up. The illusion will be complete if the index finger bears down on the end of the heap as at the beginning (Illus. 98).

98

Detection

■ Be suspicious of any distraction occurring just before or after a cut (for example, the noise of a glass falling or a chair shifting and unbalancing a player).

■ A too rapid movement in picking up is suspicious.

■ A player who has just picked up the two heaps should not keep them hidden in his hand.

■ After the two heaps have been picked up and the deal is about to begin, no suspicious noise should be heard, such as snapping or rustling.

■ After the pick-up, the dealer should not wait too long before dealing.

Second Dealing

These are the card cheat's techniques for giving bad cards to other players or for having his accomplice win. The principle is simple. Instead of dealing down the first card in the usual way, the second card is dealt in its place, or the bottom card or even a card from the middle of the pack, which eliminates the need for a shift. Most of the time, it is marked cards that tell the card sharp what movement he should execute. The speed of execution in skilful second dealing calls for many years of practice.

FIRST MANIPULATION: The Second Deal

The left hand normally holds the pack ready for the deal (Illus. 99). When the right hand approaches with the thumb and index finger ready to take a card, the thumb of the left hand slides the top card to the rear. The right thumb presses on the corner of the second card and edges it out (Illus. 100). As soon as it is out a little bit, the right index squeezes it against the thumb and pulls it completely out. The left thumb restores the first card to its normal position (Illus. 101).

99

100

101

SECOND MANIPULATION: The Second Deal

The pack is edged toward the right and the two first cards stick out sharply (Illus. 102). The middle finger of the right hand grasps the second card from underneath and slides it under the first so that it sticks out to the right (Illus. 103). The view from below shows the positions of the fingers better (Illus. 104). The right hand continues to draw the second card and put it down as though it were the first (Illus. 105).

105   106

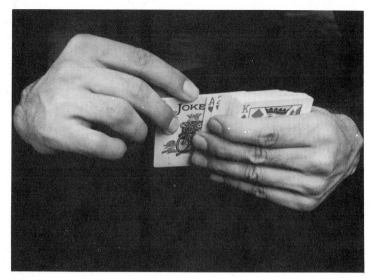

104

THIRD MANIPULATION: Dealing from the Bottom

The left hand holds the pack in the normal manner. The thumb can be held out a bit in order not to hinder the manipulation. The right hand grasps the bottom card and puts it down as though it were the first card (Illus. 106). The way in which the card is held by the right hand can be seen better from below (Illus. 107).

107

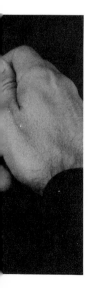

108

109

FOURTH MANIPULATION: Dealing from the Middle

The heaps have just been picked up after the cut. The fingers of the left hand, however, are keeping them apart and are beginning to pull a card out (Illus. 108). A narrow card or a crimped one can show the place where the card is to be pulled from. The right hand puts this card down as though it were the first card (Illus. 109).

Detection

■ The best way to spot this is to listen for a change of sound. The additional rubbing of cards against each other produces a different sound.

■ An unusual movement of the left thumb during the deal is a sign of second dealing.

■ A player moistening his right fingers often in dealing may be a card sharp.

■ If a player does not put the cut back in the pack but uses only the second heap in dealing he may be giving a bottom deal.

■ Any abrupt stop during the deal for any reason could be a sign of unsuccessful palming, and a new deal should be called for.

Switching Cards on the Table

For stud poker as well as for many other games, a card sharp must be able to switch a card lying on the table.

FIRST MANIPULATION: The Turn-around or Mexican Turnover

Card A is to be turned up. One of its corners is held by the index finger of the left hand. The right hand uses card B like a shovel, holding it between the thumb and index (Illus. 110). Card B is slipped under card A (Illus. 111). The right thumb releases card B and squeezes card A against the right middle finger. The tip of the right index finger holds card B in balance. The left index finger pulls away (Illus. 112). The right index tips up card B so that its face appears. Thumb and middle finger of the right hand continue to hold card A while pushing it to the left (Illus. 113). All these movements must flow smoothly in order to give the appearance that card A has been turned up by using card B, although the opposite has taken place.

110

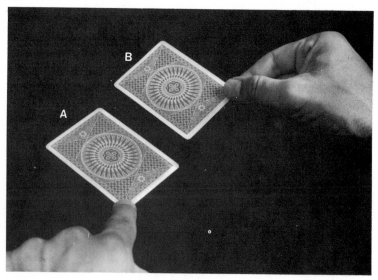

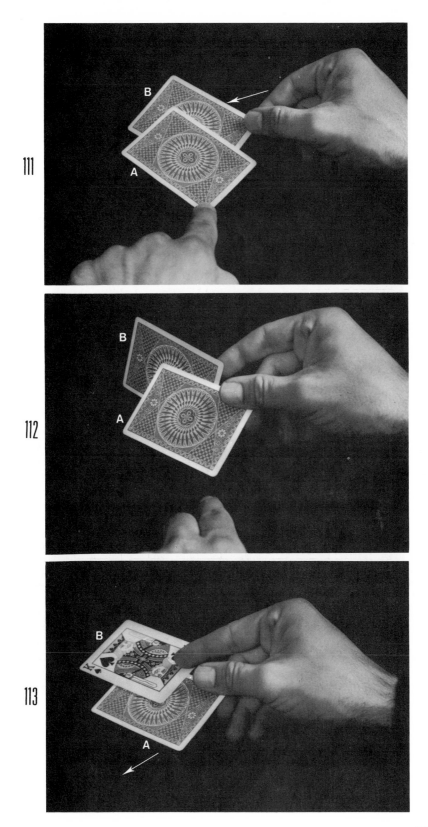

111

112

113

114

115

116

117

The right hand deals the cards in the usual way, but has palmed card A and is holding it at an angle (see chapter on Palming) (Illus. 114). At the moment of making the switch, the right index and middle fingers bend down and squeeze the top of the pack. The left thumb edges card B out slightly, ready to be switched (Illus. 115). The right thumb has just grasped card B (the palmed card held at an angle) as though to put it down on the table. The index and middle fingers are still holding card A (Illus. 116). The right hand moves slightly forward. The right index and middle fingers must unbend while holding card A, which has been turned over to show its face (Illus. 117). The right hand approaches the left hand in order to place card B on the pack (Illus. 118).

Detection

■ The hand turning a card up must be empty. The act of using another card to help has to be suspicious.

■ When a card has been turned up, the hand doing so must not come near the pack.

■ Any complicated movement in turning up a card may be dishonest.

■ Too big a movement in turning up a card is unnecessary, and therefore suspicious.

118

The Oblique Peek

Several methods make it possible to look secretly at a card on the top or bottom of the pack without being observed by the other players. If the card is useful to the card sharp, a well executed palming will enable him to get it while dealing. Knowing what the bottom card is, is a distinct advantage in gin rummy. As for the top card, knowing what it is gives a stud poker player a big advantage.

FIRST MANIPULATION: Peeking at the Bottom Card

The left thumb holds the end of the pack against the base of the left index finger. The right hand holds both ends (Illus. 119). The right hand moves the whole pack forward in the direction of the

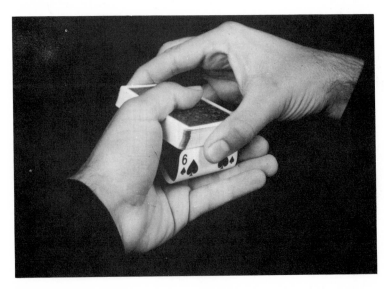

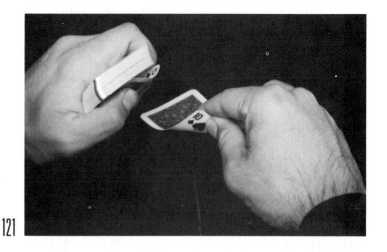

121

other players, but the base of the left index finger still holds the end of the bottom card. This end of this card is automatically bent up and the cheat can see easily that it is the Six of Spades (Illus. 120).

Second Manipulation: Peeking at the Top Card

While dealing, the cheat puts his left hand, holding the pack vertically, on the table. The right hand meanwhile picks the card up from the table (for example, in stud poker) in the "normal" manner, and the cheat can see that it is, say, the Ten of Spades (Illus. 121). During this movement, however, the left thumb pushes the top card towards the index finger, which crimps it so that the cheat can secretly see the corner near the index finger: Five of Spades, for example.

Third Manipulation: Peeking at the Top Card

When shuffling the cards in the American style (riffle shuffling, or overhand shuffling), the cheat can easily keep back the top card. It takes only a fraction of a second to spot the King of Spades by raising the corner of the card a little bit higher than it would be normally (Illus. 122).

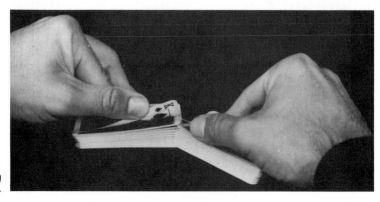

122

Detection

■ Normally, the pack should not be held too long in the hand, unless something improper is going on. A player fiddling nervously with the pack before dealing can be peeking.

■ When there is no longer a reason for holding the pack in the hand, it should be placed on the table.

■ Cards should never be lifted too high by the player who is shuffling.

■ A player concealing the palm of his hand too carefully may have a mirror there so that he can get a look without manipulating.

Palming

This manipulation is common to all card games. It consists of keeping one or more cards in the hand without letting the others see them. Each palming position corresponds to a natural position of the hand, which makes it easier to conceal the card. Card sharps with big hands are particularly fond of this technique. That is why the French gambling authorities increased the size of the cards used in casinos, making palming practically impossible (see Chapter 10). You should study carefully the movements that facilitate each type of palming.

123

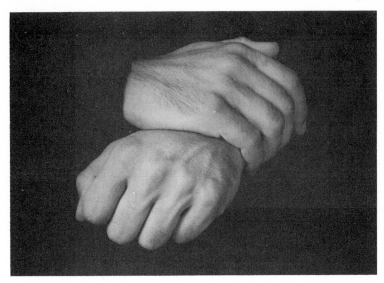

124

FIRST POSITION: Classic palming (Illus. 123)

The card is chiefly held at point A in Illus. 123 by the tip of the
little finger, and at point B by the muscle at the base of the thumb.
The cheat can cross his arms or put the hand holding the card on the
wrist of the other arm (Illus. 124). The hand holding the card can
toy in a mechanical fashion with an object lying on the table such as
a cigarette case (Illus. 125).

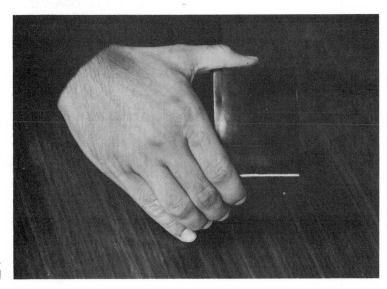

125

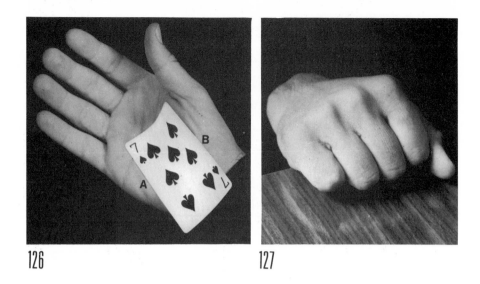

126   127

SECOND POSITION: The Gambler's Palm (Illus. 126)

You can easily proceed from the classic method of palming to this one. The card is drawn towards the wrist. It is held at point A and point B by the thenar and hypothenar muscles. This is the most commonly used method. The cheat can keep his fist closed on the edge of the table (Illus. 127). He can even open out the fingers flat on the edge of the table (Illus. 128).

THIRD POSITION: Palming on the Slant (Illus. 129)

The angle at which the other players cannot see the card is much smaller than in the other positions. It is the thumb that holds the card against the palm. By this method, several cards can easily be held. The pretext of holding a pencil in no way hinders palming (Illus. 130). Seen from the front, the pencil accounts for the lightly closed position of the hand (Illus. 131).

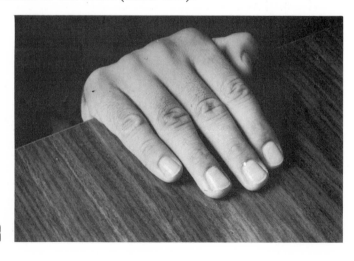

128

129

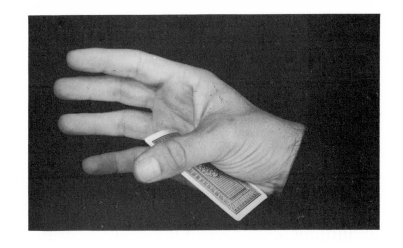

130

131

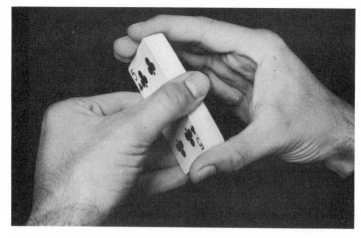

132

First Manipulation: Classic Two-Hand Palming

The pack is held in the left hand by the sides. The right hand holds the ends as though to straighten them (Illus. 132). The tips of the fingers of the right hand push the top card from the pack (Illus. 133). When this card sticks out about a centimetre (2/5ths of an inch) the fingers press on the end to make it arch up against the palm (Illus. 134).

Second Manipulation: Classic Two-Hand Palming

The pack is held in the left hand. The right hand presses against the top card in a diagonal movement. The corner of the pack serves as a support for the top card which has just been pushed against the palm (Illus. 135).

Third Manipulation: Classic One-Hand Palming

The pack is held by the ends with the right hand. The little finger presses against the first card, shoving it slightly forward (Illus. 136 and 137). The end of the pack serves as a support, so the little finger can assume a position that will lever the card into the palm, hiding it from the view of the other players (Illus. 138).

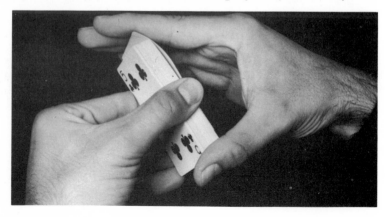

133

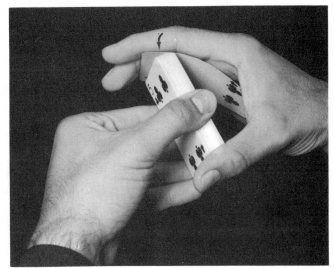

134

135

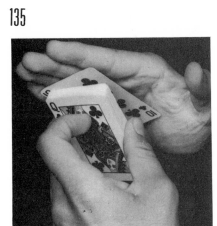

136

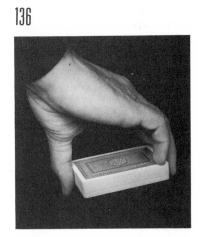

137

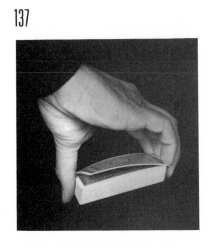

138

139

140

141

FOURTH MANIPULATION: Palming the Bottom Card with Two Hands

The pack is held by the ends in the right hand. The left hand fingers are bent over the bottom card (Illus. 139). The tips of the fingers of the left hand are pressing on this card. The fingers continue their movement (Illus. 140) and place the card against the right palm (Illus. 141). This is an example of classic palming.

86

142

143

144

FIFTH MANIPULATION: Palming the Bottom Card with One Hand

The pack is held by both ends with the right hand (Illus. 142). The fingers bend and the card is now held only by the index and thumb. The ring finger presses on the bottom card and displaces it to the side (Illus. 143).

The middle finger slides over the top of the pack and swings the pack forward to allow the card to pass toward the palm (Illus. 144).

145

The ball of the thumb grips the obliquely palmed card while laying down the pack (Illus. 145).

SIXTH MANIPULATION: A Trick Ring

The card is simply slid under a little metal strip attached to a special ring. Palming clearly is very easy with this simple device (Illus. 146).

146

Detection

■ You can suspect palming when a player holds his hand stiff or his fingers squeezed together in an exaggerated way.

■ Similarly, if a player holds an object between his fingers—a pen, matchbox, etc.

■ If the thumb is out of sight, it could mean that a card is being palmed obliquely.

■ The preferred moment for palming is when the cards are up and the edges of the pack are straightened.

Returning Palmed Cards

When an accomplice signals to a card sharp by an invisible method that he needs a certain card or cards, the card sharp first has to obtain them (by a special device), then palm them and finally, get them into the pack without being seen by the other players. It could also be a matter of placing an additional card on the pack or one that has been kept out secretly. The pretext is always that of picking up the pack to hand it to another player or to shuffle.

FIRST MANIPULATION: Two Hands without a Support

The left hand picks up the pack while the right hand approaches, palming a card as it does (Illus. 147). The right hand has just put the card in the pack under the pretext of straightening out the cards with the tips of the fingers (Illus. 148).

147

148

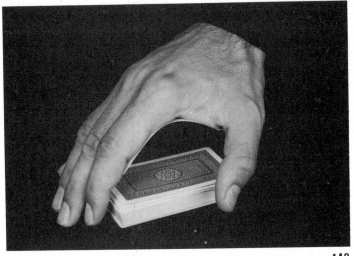

149

Second Manipulation: With One Hand while Picking Up

The right hand, holding the palmed card, grasps the pack and eases toward the palmed card. At the moment of lifting the pack, the card is released (Illus. 149).

Third Manipulation: Restoring the Cut

The left hand restores the cut, leaving the two heaps somewhat out of line with one another. The right hand continues to hold the palmed card (Illus. 150). Under the pretext of straightening out the pack, the right hand draws nearer and plants the palmed card while sliding the upper heap into place (Illus. 151).

150

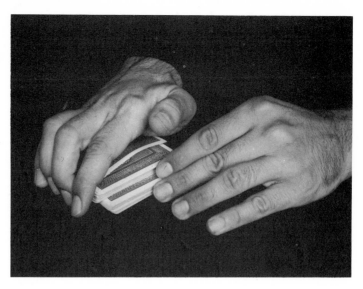

151

Detection

- The act of needlessly picking up the pack to pass it to another player, instead of pushing it across the table, is suspicious.
- When a player places a pack on the table, if the first card is slightly curved, there is a good chance that this card has just been added.
- You can easily discourage a card sharp from using this method by counting the cards at the beginning of the game and recounting them from time to time.

152 To Las Vegas, world capital of gambling, come many card sharps, eager to try out their own systems.

7. The World's Greatest Cheats

I would like you to meet some cheats that I consider the "greatest." My criterion is not that they have a great deal of money or that one of their manipulations shows incredible ingenuity. Instead, it is the fact that they have cheated in an original way, over a long period of time and with great intelligence. They have never been caught by other players or by the police. Their psychology is so great that their methods seem infallible. They have been willing, by virtue of a friendly feeling toward me, to reveal their techniques and way of life to me. I promised them, of course, to cover their tracks by changing their names, as well as certain characteristics. Any similarity to the name of an honest card player or with another card sharp is pure coincidence.

Furthermore, I mention their native countries, but these tricksters are international and one cannot attribute a nationality to them other than "Greek," a term applied in France and elsewhere to card cheats that came into use following a court scandal that occured during the reign of Louis XIV.

Actually, a soldier of fortune, Greek by birth, Theodore Apoulos by name, won a great fortune at cards. In 1686, at the residence of Marshal de Villeroy, some guests were playing lansquenet (a game similar to "Banker and Broker," in which any number can play against a banker, placing bets on single cards). A gentleman from Poitou, who was in a bad humor because he had lost a great deal of money, was struck by an idea. He grabbed Theodore Apoulos by both wrists and started shaking the Greek's wide lace sleeves. Out fell a whole assortment of devices for cheating that were quite advanced for that period. The "knave" was sentenced to penal servitude. Since that time card sharps in France have often been referred to as "Greeks." However, I never ran across a card sharp in the fair land of Greece.

153 The millionaires of Capetown play
stud poker with diamonds as stakes.

The Capetown Diamond Broker

None of the poker players in Capetown know for sure whether Mel Fergson was rich or not before he started playing cards. They all had known him for a long time as an important dealer in precious stones. Today, his fortune is such that he is one of a small group of players who bet only with diamonds. The group gets together once a week in a room at the club that has practically been set up for them (Illus. 153). While the gentlemen are playing, their ladies stroll about the club grounds, in the midst of monkeys! The club is situated outside the city, a little before the Cape. The atmosphere of the place, unique in the world, had drawn me there and I really did not expect to discover a card sharp in such an environment. However, I am obliged to yield to the facts. Mel Fergson is a

95

Grand Master. He has no need of money. He cheats purely for pleasure, and his technique includes an innovation which has led me to nickname him the "Rubber Band King."

Mel employs a number of classic methods, but most of the time he creates a set-up in shuffling the cards that allows his accomplice to win. The sole preparation involved consists of wedging a tiny bit of rubber band under the nail of his right middle finger. Just when he's about to place a heavy stake, he picks up the cards to shuffle them and manages to place three similar cards—say three Kings on the top of the pack. He rapidly shuffles the rest of the cards while carrying out the following manipulation: he slips the 6 top cards one by one into his left hand. He puts this group back on the pack. He repeats the same operation with the 4 top cards. Then, again, with the next 9 cards, and lastly with 4 cards.

He asks the player to his right to cut. Then with the tips of the fingers of his right hand, he taps on the pile of cards (heap) nearest himself, and says, "cut again." This natural-seeming movement has enabled him to place, unobserved, the bit of rubber band on the half-pack. Even after a second cut, a slight break caused by the bit of rubber is enough to enable Mel Fergson to bypass the cut. The order of the cards remains the same. Fergson deals the cards in the usual way. The accomplice at his left gets the three Kings. All our card sharp has left to do is later on to split the diamonds won in the game with his secret partner.

In spite of his skill and coolness, Fergson had reason to get pretty scared of me due to an unforeseen incident. The players had decided to have a sandwich break. No one could have guessed that Mel was ready to cheat as soon as the game resumed. He had two Jacks up his right sleeve, all the while munching on his sandwich. However, I had caught on because, thanks to my keen eyesight, I detected an overly tense nerve on the back of his hand. Abruptly one of the honest players picked up the pack and began to count the cards mechanically. It was simply that he had eaten faster than the others and was looking for something to fill in the time. I saw Fergson turn pale. The absence of the two Jacks was surely going to raise suspicions and lead to a search of the players. Mel very calmly placed the cards against his sandwich, turned the sandwich over and proceeded to eat sandwich and Jacks. By the time the cards had been counted a second time and the absence of the two cards had been established, Mel had finished his sandwich and swallowed the cards. He joined in the search for the missing Jacks along with his fellow players. Of course they didn't find them, and no one was searched, for cheating seemed senseless in such a place.

This incident provided me with a good opportunity, when a week later, I happened to be with Mel Fergson in private. I let him know what I had observed in a humorous fashion, using a card trick. I handed him my cards and showed him that my hands were empty. Then, a magic gesture and two jacks popped out of my mouth.

Mel appreciated my discretion and offered me his friendship, to the point of allowing me to write about his incredible feat of *sang-froid*.

The Patriarch of Las Vegas

When you arrive at the airport in Las Vegas, there is nothing to distinguish it from other United States airports of the same size, except for the stifling heat.

You disappear into an air-conditioned taxi and head into town, or shall I say toward "The Strip." The illusion is total: the residential areas, where the casino employees live, are off to the side and are wholly screened by large casinos with multi-colored façades that are illuminated night and day. They are lined up next to each other on both sides of an immensely wide avenue.

On my first trip there, the taxi dropped me in front of my casino-hotel. No welcome, no porter. I had to carry my bags in the direction of the reception desk. To get there you have to cross a room full of slot machines. As a rule, after a few minutes, you start to tire and you stop, face to face with a slot machine. While catching your breath, you put a coin in the machine, and then another, and another, and soon you've forgotten about your suitcases. Some players, if they win, stay on the winning machine for three or four hours. They have drinks and sandwiches brought to them. These casinos are open 24 hours a day and there are always people playing.

Immune from this kind of temptation, I continue on my way. You usually have to pay for your room in advance. They even ask you if you wish to leave your return ticket in the hotel safe. In the early days when I visited Las Vegas, the hotels had quite reasonable rates, considering the luxuriousness of the rooms. Actually, nothing was expensive in Las Vegas. The restaurants were excellent and were quite reasonable. But the biggest surprise was the entertainment. For a nominal charge, you could watch a show whose cost could in no way be covered by the admission price—many regular customers were even there as guests of the hotel management. Of course, it was the games in the casino that paid for all this (Illus. 154). Today, the hotels and restaurants are not so reasonable—they charge rates about the same as other resort cities.

154 At the Circus Circus Casino, a player
has every guarantee of honest play.

Blackjack, poker, and craps are still the leading games. For the
first week of my visit, I was unable to get any information about
cheating. But my direct and precise questions aroused a growing
curiosity. One day I was approached by a young man who invited
me to dinner and asked what my profession was. I declared, "a
sleight-of-hand artist doing research on the basics of card sharping."
He asked me to demonstrate my technical competence in handling
cards. I willingly gave an example. He seemed surprised and
admiring, asked me my name and where I was staying, and then
left, promising to introduce me to a great specialist in the next few
days.

After several days I thought that he had forgotten and I took to
spending my time with French entertainers appearing in some
of the big shows, and whom I was happy to run into again.

On the fourth day, as promised when we met, he sent a message to my hotel, making an appointment for that evening. I was naturally there on time. The young man said he was going to present me, in a private room, to the "Patriarch of Card Sharps," Sam Barker. He went on to say that Barker was 75 years old but didn't look it and was incontestably the No. 1 specialist in card sharping. I frankly admit that I had never heard of him. For me, the greatest American specialists were prestidigitators who limited themselves to giving spectacular demonstrations of trickery.

The first contact was very cold. The gentleman was in evening dress. He simply took a pack of cards from his pocket and asked me to demonstrate some manoeuvres. I understood that I was being tested. Having prepared myself for this eventuality, I did my best and carried it off in good form. Faced with these difficult feats, the young man shook his head and turned toward Sam Barker. The latter remained immobile, merely saying in an even voice, "More."

After about 45 minutes, I was worn out and was beginning to feel a maddening anguish at the thought of going on with these demonstrations. Sam Barker must have sensed this. He smiled for the first time, congratulated me and ordered three whiskies. He explained to me that he was wary of the many card players who only wanted to learn a few of his tricks, and then declared that he was going to show me his specialties. It took 5 hours, during which he drank 35 shots of whisky. He nonetheless stayed in top form.

For my part, I was exhausted, and I had only drunk a few glasses of fruit juice. But what a spectacle! Such superhuman feats truly require 30 years of practice. A whole psychology by any test. He furthermore gave me permission to describe one of his tricks in this book, but I shall not tell you which one it is. But the most fantastic thing is still his personal experience in the Las Vegas scene.

Sam Barker was suspected of being a card sharp by the management of a big casino, about 30 years earlier. Sam cheated at poker by fixing cards so that an accomplice would win. Up to this point, the story is commonplace, but the rest of it is out of this world.

The casino management, aware that it had to deal with an exceptional cheat, a man possessing elegance, refinement and total mastery, offered him a rather unusual job. It consisted of his becoming a croupier and cheating, not to make certain patrons lose (this the casinos never do, since their normal take is ample), but to make some of them win. A "good year-round customer" comes to Las Vegas for a week, and loses everything the first night. He is so disappointed that he may leave the next morning, having spent only one-seventh of what he might have. Similarly, if he loses too heavily on the last night, he will wait a month or two before coming back, instead of showing up sooner. Therefore he has to be made to win. And so, for 25 years, Sam carried out this assignment to perfection.

His favorite was blackjack. He used marked cards and practiced second dealing with virtuosity. He has been in retirement for 5 years and lives a very agreeable life at the expense of the casino. All they ask of him is an occasional little private demonstration for some king or prince who is passing through. And now you will ask me who has taken his place. Nobody. The casinos have numerous compensations to offer unlucky players. Free airline tickets, free accommodations on their next visit, among others. In any case, the intoxication produced by the atmosphere of gambling is such that the player feels a need to come back, as if he were drugged. But for 25 years, Sam Barker bent chance to his will, all the while giving great joy to card players.

The Boeing 747 Commuter

Along with many European magicians my dream was to visit the Magic Castle one day, the Hollywood temple of prestidigitation. In this extraordinary place, a perfect reproduction of a Victorian mansion, the best American magicians meet and put on a show of the highest quality. The great originality lies in the presentation of table tricks in a little amphitheatre constructed especially for this purpose. The host and manager at this distinctive cabaret-restaurant is called Bill Larsen. He is very demanding as to the technique of the magicians he engages, and only allows club members to sit in the audience. The latter are not necessarily amateur sleight-of-hand artists, but must in any case be magic enthusiasts in order to accept the conditions of this gathering: definite hours for the sessions, obligatory dark suits and ties, and a universe of surprises and magic tricks.

The third floor is given over to a library whose books on magic are only available to confirmed practitioners of the art. Presiding over the library is the "Professor," Dai Vernon. This old gentleman remains one of the most brilliant card experts in the whole world. With the greatest courtesy, he receives foreign specialists and introduces them to his American friends. Of the latter, Larry Jennings is by far the most amazing due to his absolute mastery of the most difficult manipulations. Naturally, at the castle the members communicate with one another primarily with their hands and by means of card tricks. The systematic analysis of all forms of trickery in this environment is a unique factor in developing new illusions. Therefore it seemed a bit odd when, on one of my trips to Los Angeles in a Boeing 747, I saw a cheat using an extraordinary technique, and one so novel that no member of the Magic Castle knew of it.

The regular Paris-Los Angeles flight by Boeing 747 has one stop for fuel at Montreal. Between Paris and Montreal, the passengers get to know one another, in spite of the deafening noise made by this giant of the air. First-class passengers can go upstairs to a lounge that is quite well sound-proofed. There is a bar there and often a card game is in progress. From Montreal to Los Angeles, the games become much more serious and the stakes are often much higher. By chance I happened to run into a certain card player twice on this same flight. I observed him closely. He cheated right before my eyes. He no doubt earned his living in this way, for I learned from the hostess that he had a seat booked on this flight once a week, but always on a different day. In a sort of way he was the only "commuter" on this Boeing 747.

Of German origin, Erik Farber looked like a top executive, with his attaché case full of files. At first he grumbled about all the work piled up on him, but he soon lost the desire to work and ended up in the card game. With his sportsman's physique and open face, Erik appealed to people, all the more so since he was very generous in buying drinks for others. The first time I noticed him, he won at gin rummy, and the second he piled up big winnings at poker. The cheating technique he used on the first flight was very simple, but very effective, while the second time the ingeniousness of his method flabbergasted me.

For the game of gin rummy, Erik Farber used his own pack, but he could just as easily have used someone else's. His only secret manipulation was to take the pack of cards out of its case, leaving one card still inside. You have to realize that the absence of that one card gives a clear advantage to the player who knows about it. For example, if the card held back were the Seven of Diamonds, the customary combinations are not possible, since the following are eliminated: 5, 6, 7 of Diamonds, 6, 7, 8 of Diamonds, and 7, 8, 9 of Diamonds. The cheat thus has several advantages. He knows that the combination 7, 7, 7 is not too likely and that any combination involving the 7 of Diamonds is impossible. Furthermore, his opponent, unaware of this, may decide to try for one of the impossible combinations. Our card sharp, being a good player, has made full use of his advantage, and won.

The amount of money involved wasn't very big, but then neither was the risk. What could be more excusable than a card that stayed stuck in the case? The only way I knew what he was doing was through observing the special way in which he moved his index finger when opening the case. This is a movement that I use myself when doing a trick in which I leave a card selected by a spectator inside the case, without his knowing it.

The poker game dumbfounded me, for the method used was incredibly bold. The game went on as usual until it was announced that the plane was approaching Los Angeles. All the passengers had already ordered more drinks and the steward was slow in bringing them. The card players decided to have one last game. It was Erik Farber's turn to deal. The pack had just been shuffled by one of the three honest players and Erik was holding it in his left hand. The steward arrived abruptly, holding his tray in his left hand, excused himself for disturbing them, and announced that he could serve them no more drinks after this. He took a glass of whisky from the tray and handed it to the player seated at Erik's left. Quite naturally, the tray hid the pack of cards in Erik's hand for a moment. Because of the rapidity and precision of this movement, for an instant I had the crazy notion that maybe the pack had been switched.

Erik dealt the cards. Very big stakes were put up by Erik and an American player. Everyone put down his hand. The American had four of a kind, which Erik beat with a straight flush. This extraordinary game looked suspicious to me and while the steward was busying himself behind the bar, I had a strong urge to go and take a look at his tray. At that moment a hostess appeared and asked him to help her with a passenger who had become ill below. This was the moment I was waiting for. Telling those near me that I didn't feel well, I headed toward the lavatory, then crouched down like a thief and came back behind the bar. I opened all the little cabinets where the bar utensils were kept and was intrigued to find a white nylon pouch. Afraid that I would be discovered, I grabbed it without looking inside and repaired to the lavatory. Naturally I found the pack of cards inside the pouch, as well as some little containers of wax to be used for other trickery. I was not wrong, a switch had definitely taken place and this steward accomplice was one of the most skilled manipulators that I ever knew. I kept the pack. While leaving the plane, I even complimented Erik Farber on his marvelous luck.

A few months later, I had occasion to take that same flight. There were only some children playing beggar-my-neighbor, who were close to coming to blows, they were such awful players. Erik Farber was not there. Neither was the steward. A new employee told me that the one I had known had asked for a reassignment to another route. However, I found a hostess with whom I had previously struck up an acquaintance, and asked her if Erik Farber was still booking his weekly seat on the flight. She replied that he had dropped out of sight. There was no longer a commuter on the Boeing 747.

The Italian Perfumer

Tall, dark and athletic, Luigi Giaccoto is the very image of an Italian playboy. He runs a small perfume business in Rome whose profits can't amount to very much, but his main line of work lies elsewhere. Luigi is an excellent bridge player. He is very much in demand and plays in all the main tournaments. He also always wins. He can thus live on a scale of exceptional luxury. "This is worth the trouble of cheating a tiny bit," he confided to me, while lounging beside his swimming pool.

I shall not devote too much space to his speciality, for it is not really original. Lots of bridge players cheat in very much the same way, with less success perhaps. The only difference between them and Luigi is a thing called an I.Q. Hats off to Luigi. Even without cheating, he is a master player.

Since entire books have been written on the fine points and subtleties of bridge, it is not easy to explain briefly the principles and methods of cheating applicable to each one of them. It is enough to state that it is the card sharp's business to learn what is in his partner's hand and to let the partner know what is in his. Electronic devices are used for this purpose by many card sharps, but Luigi Giaccoto prefers the refinements of an "audio-visual" code, a classic method but one that is still good.

A very simple example will illustrate the subtlety of this method. Luigi bids Hearts, which means therefore that he has five cards of this suit. Two simultaneous actions escape the notice of the opponents but not of the partner, who is watching for them. The first is visual—Luigi has placed his cigarette on the ashtray which means that he doesn't have honors. The second clue is audible. A slight clearing of the throat before bidding means "I don't have the Ace." Minor gestures and noises of this sort can be used in an infinite number of combinations to transmit exact information on the cards he is holding. And even if the players are suspicious, how can they discern the meaning of cards, fingers, cigarette, whisky glass, etc., when these are held or placed in a certain position? For good bridge players, the advantages of this system are enormous, and needless to say, our perfumer makes maximum use of them.

Nonetheless, I have tricked Luigi Giaccoto, but not at bridge. When the game is over, Luigi always asks a few people to be his guests at a restaurant. And on the way there, he always happens to notice an old playing card stuck in a grating or in the wheel of a bicycle. Luigi calls attention to the card, whose soiled face is not too clearly discernible. However, he does not identify the card by suit or value. Nonetheless his new friends can make out the King of Spades. They continue on their way, and when they get to the next corner, our sharpie says, "Funny, seeing that King of Hearts in the street." One of the others says, "No, it was the King of Spades." An argument starts. Luigi says he will bet money that it was the King of Hearts. Someone takes him up on it. They go back to the spot where they saw the card. The unlucky bettor snatches up the card. It is, of course, the King of Hearts. The loser pays up without protest. Since Luigi is buying the champagne as well as the supper, the subject is dropped.

The time that I was present at one of these performances, I felt certain that he had an accomplice who switched cards before the group came back to check. The next day, when the card games were over, I kept out of sight and followed Luigi and his companions. Was he going to repeat his stratagem? Yes. He drew the attention of his new friends to a card at the foot of a lamp post and then they went on their way. A woman then appeared close by the lamp post and bent over as though to adjust something on her shoe, and while doing this, replaced the card with another. Then the charming confederate straightened up and proceeded on her way in a normal manner. Luckily, everything happened just as I had foreseen. I went up to the lamp post, picked up the second card and put a third one in its place. I quickly withdrew and hid in the shade of a doorway, to wait. I didn't have long. A few moments later, Luigi and company reappeared. The intended victim picked up the card and burst out laughing, complimenting Luigi on his sense of humor. Mystified, Luigi took the card and looked at it. It was a plain white card on which was written a brief message: "You lose."

The Belgian Bridge Cheats

For ten years a group of card sharps has been working trains. They are a very strong team. Arnold is the leader—he's the one who manipulates the cards and directs the others. Bertrand is the one who finds the "suckers." Claude pretends to be on the side of the sucker and consoles him when he loses.

Our three sharpers make a habit of boarding the train at Brussels, going toward Ostend. They take seats in an empty compartment; Arnold and Bertrand take the two window seats, on either side of the little table; Claude sits down next to the corridor. They spread their baggage over the seats to make it look as though the compartment is fully occupied.

A quarter of an hour before the train is due to leave, Bertrand goes into the first-class compartment and asks if anyone would like to make a fourth at bridge. If a passenger is interested, Bertrand takes him back to the card sharps' compartment and has him sit opposite Arnold and next to himself. Arnold then calls to Claude, who is reading a newspaper and is naturally acting as though he doesn't know them, and asks him if he would be willing to play, since there are now four people present. Claude acts unenthusiastic and says, "You know, I'm not very good at bridge and I'd make a poor partner for anyone." Arnold insists and finally Claude agrees and sits with them.

Arnold then brings out a pack of cards and says, "If you wish, we could make the game more interesting by playing one franc a point. It's not a question of winning money, or losing it, but just the same, it makes it more appealing." Everyone agrees and Arnold deals thirteen cards to each player. The pack is counted and recounted, but there is a card missing—the Six of Clubs. They stoop down, get up, look all over and still don't find it. Claude gets up abruptly and says, "Sorry, gentlemen, but there's no way we can play." The sucker starts to get up and leave, but Arnold says to them, "Wait, since we're all here anyway, I know a little game using 32 cards. It's a lot of fun and it will help us pass the time." Everybody returns to his seat.

Arnold explains the game: The value of the cards is in descending order—Ace, King, Queen, Jack, etc. The banker deals three cards to each player. The banker holds the rest of the pack. Each player has a turn at being banker.

The banker starts with a small stake of one franc. Each player takes his turn and has the right to make three plays with the hand he holds. The aim is of course to win the stake, or pot. To win you need a card higher than the one the banker turns up, but of the same suit. For example, if the first card the banker turns up is the Seven of Spades, the player loses his stake if he has no Spades in his hand. But he still has two more shots. However, he has to double his stake, since he already has lost once. If he wins, he picks up the pot, and the banker puts a franc out to start a new one, and the game continues in this order. The round is over when the cards are used up and the banker picks up the pot if there is one.

This game looks simple and amusing and they decide to play a practice game first. Bertrand is the banker and he shuffles and has the pack cut. At this point, Claude starts talking to the sucker to distract his attention for a few seconds. While he is doing this, Bertrand switches the pack for another that is stacked.

Bertrand deals three cards to each player. No one has a strong enough hand for a stake and everybody passes (there is one franc in the pot). Bertrand deals the cards again. Claude has a somewhat weak hand—a Jack, a Ten and a King—but he decides to play it. He loses and plays again. He loses again and is about to go for the third time, when Arnold asks to see his hand. Claude shows it to him and Arnold says, "Well, in your situation, I wouldn't play it." But Claude won't listen and places a stake. He loses. The sucker is beginning to follow and can hardly wait to play, since he has an Ace, a King and a Jack in his hand. He doesn't hesitate. He wins, and they all begin playing in earnest. Before the end of the second game, somebody asks the sucker where he's getting off the train. "Ghent," he says, which means they have half an hour. There's time for a bit of fun. . .

The sucker has won 32 francs by the end of the second game. Although he does not normally play for money, he's getting more and more interested in the game. There are still fifteen minutes left before the train pulls into the station at Ghent. This is the moment to stick the sucker. Once more the pack is switched, unknown to the sucker, for another one that will enable the tricksters to see how he will react to bigger stakes. Arnold is the banker. He puts down two francs in order to swell the pot faster. When it is the sucker's turn to play, there are already 128 francs in the pot, since the intervening players lost. The sucker now has in his hand a King, an Ace and a Queen, but he hesitates to play since the amount involved is so large. Finally he decides, but Arnold tells him to keep his money in his hand in case there's a verification. The sucker wins and at the end of the game, he asks that the first stake put out by the banker in the next game be five francs.

The pack for the next game, of course, has been stacked. Bertrand and Arnold play first and lose, after raising the pot to 640 francs. The sucker has two Aces and a King in his hand and is all the more impatient to play since he has to get off in ten minutes. It is Arnold's turn to hold the money. The sucker immediately puts down 640 francs and loses, for he does not have the right suit. He plays again, this time he must double the stake, making it 1,280 francs. Again he loses, his King taken by an Ace which Claude turns up. He doesn't hesitate to try a third time with his Ace, but once more Claude shows him another suit. The pot, now up to 5,120 francs, is soon doubled after the next deal, for the sucker has the last Ace in his hand and knows that he cannot be beaten by a higher card. However, he forgets that he can be beaten by another suit, and that is just what happens.

Confident to the end, the sucker bets once more, but loses when Claude turns up a higher card. At this point, the sucker says he's pulling out of the game. Saying that he understands very well why, Claude turns up the card that would have come into play if the sucker had taken a third try. With an angelic smile, Claude says, "You see how perseverance pays. If you'd gone for a third you'd have won." Claude simply forgets to add that the card he just turned up came off the bottom, not the top, of the pack. But the sucker didn't notice, since his nerves were on edge and he suddenly realized that the train was coming into the station. He grabs his suitcase, mutters goodbye and jumps off the train, all the while trying to keep his hat from blowing off. Claude's eyes follow him to see whether he has realized that he was swindled and is looking for a policeman. However, he sees the sucker give a friendly wave in their direction, as he gets into a taxi.

The King of the Track

Roger Baudinot never works in winter, since it is too cold for him then to practice his profession. Our man is, in fact, an out-of-doors card sharp. In good weather, he is to be found daily at one of the Paris tracks—Auteuil, Longchamp, or Vincennes. He never leaves the Paris area, where he was born. He wears the outfit of a confirmed trackgoer—cap, raincoat, turtleneck. This and his eager face give him the look of a gambler who can always charm an occasional adversary.

He bets moderately in every race except the last. He doesn't stay for that, but leaves the stands ahead of the crowd and joins three or four confederates who are waiting for him on one of the paths surrounding the track. His friends help him to set up a cardboard

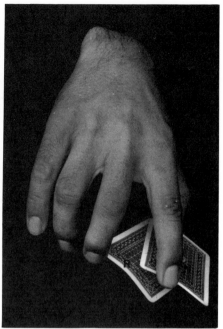

<table>
<tr><td>155</td><td>156</td></tr>
</table>

carton that will serve as a card table. Roger Baudinot is now ready for business. The tools of his trade are lying on top of the carton—two black cards and one red. His accomplices merge into the stream of people coming out of the track. They will be the first to stop and play.

The game is simple. The banker-trickster shuffles the three cards. The other player has to keep his eyes on the red card. If he thinks he knows which one it is, he places a bet with Roger. This game, called *bonneteau* in France, is known in English as the "three-card trick" or "three-card monte." If a Queen is used in place of a red card, the game is called "Find the Lady." A whole series of ploys make it possible for the sharpie and his friends to fleece a victim. Before we look at these tactics in detail, let's first take note of the moves that are at the base of this trickery.

The three cards are slightly crimped at the outset, hence the name *bonneteau,* suggesting the curve of a bonnet or cap. First let us look at the key movement in this trick.

The card sharp holds two cards in his right hand, one almost lying on top of the other (Illus. 155). The red card is on the bottom, held between the thumb and the middle finger. The black card is on top, between the thumb and the index finger. At the moment of dropping the red (lower) card, the index finger moves away from

157

the middle finger, releasing the black card, which falls to the table instead of the red (Illus. 156). The red should even be drawn back slightly over the black, so that it appears that there is no sideways movement. The speed of this switch gives the illusion that it is actually the red card that is lying on the table, when in fact it is the black (Illus. 157). The chain of actions making up this manoeuvre is so skilfully presented that it completely escapes the notice of the victim.

The card sharp shows the three cards face up. The red one is in the middle (Illus. 158). He turns the cards face down. The red card

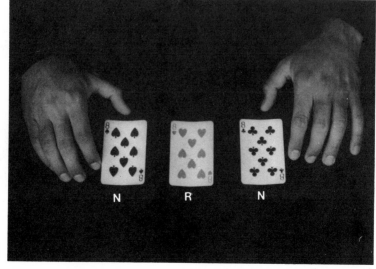

158

stays in the middle (Illus. 159). His right hand picks up the first black card (on the card sharp's right) and shows it around (Illus. 160). His right hand has just put the black card up against the red, but leaving a slight space between the two cards. The card sharp

161

turns them up saying: "Here's the red" (Illus. 161). The card sharp executes the secret manoeuvre and puts down the black card (Illus. 162). The red card is still held in the right hand but the sucker is quite sure that it is a black card. The right hand moves

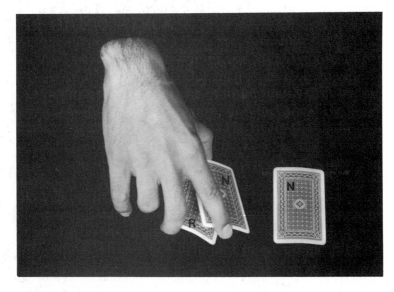

162

toward the second black card and picks it up (Illus. 163). The card sharp turns up the two cards after placing them side by side on the table. "Here's a black one," he announces (Illus. 164). He repeats the secret manoeuvre. The red is put down in place of the black (Illus. 165). The right hand moves aside and puts down the remaining card on the card sharp's right (Illus. 166). If this sequence of movements is precise and well co-ordinated, the sucker will always bet on one of the two black cards, thinking it's the red.

164

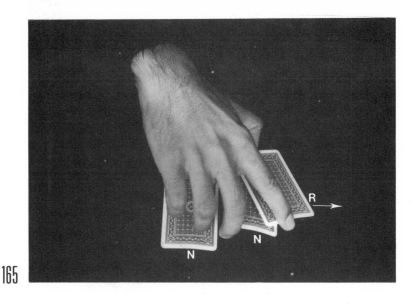

Of course, this crooked play is only used at the moment of fleecing the victim. Up until then the accomplices play, win and to make a sizeable bet ask a hesitant player to match their stakes. The sucker wins, once, twice, and then bets heavily and loses.

Since this game is illegal, at this point one of the confederates shouts "Look over there!" While the card sharp looks around to see if there is anything to this warning, another accomplice discreetly bends one of the corners of the red card, nudging the sucker as he does it so that the latter will see what he's doing. Roger

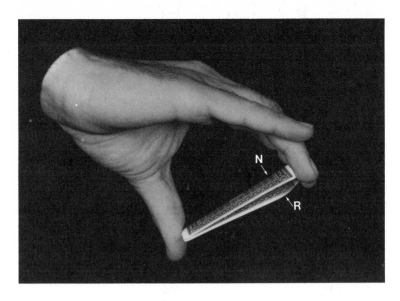

167

turns around and the game continues. The accomplice bets and loses. The sucker tells himself that he'll soon be able to make up his losses. Next time round, he puts up a large stake. The card sharp picks up the cards as usual. The red card with the crimped corner is on the bottom (Illus. 167). But before laying the cards out, Roger secretly flattens the crimped corner of the red card with the aid of his middle finger and crimps the black card with the aid of his ring finger (Illus. 168). The sucker then turns up the card he thinks is the red one and sees that the crimped card is black. He realizes that he has been had. It's too late. If he spends too much time deciding what stand to take, Roger's accomplices will push

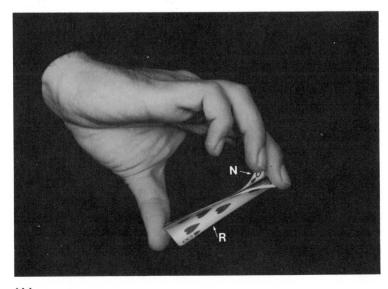

168

him aside and install another sucker in his place. If he demands his money back, the accomplice, a big, beefy type, will convince him to drop it and will even go so far as to treat him as a crook. Most of the time, the victim doesn't complain to the police. That night at dinner he will tell the family that a pickpocket relieved him of his wallet, without his knowing it.

As for Roger Baudinot, he doesn't hang around. In order to get home, he boards a bus full of trackgoers also homeward bound. On the bus, all alone, without accomplices, he plays "Banker and Broker." This game is very simple. Two or three can play it. Everybody cuts and shows the card he's cut. The one with highest card picks up the stakes. As to be expected, dear Roger cheats. Even with a pack of cards belonging to another player, he can cut at the card he wants. By simply crimping or bending a corner, he can be sure of winning. The bus ride is over soon. The moment the bus arrives in the middle of Paris, the racing enthusiasts start to disperse, but our card sharp is the most adept at disappearing.

Roger Baudinot makes such a good living that he goes to Brazil regularly on vacation. He comes back after three or four months and entertains his friends at the track with fascinating stories of his journey. A few nasty types assert that he spends his vacations in jail. People really are awful. To be sure, Baudinot always comes back with no sign of a tan. But let's not be skeptical. Roger is merely afraid of the sun, which must be a burden to an open-air cheat.

The Princess of Macao

The Far East is where one can observe the most refined cheating. Moreover, it's a woman that practices it. But not just any woman. An authentic princess whose family lived in Canton before the Communist Revolution. Since then, our princess has lived in Hong Kong, keeping up an appearance of wealth: a richly embroidered Chinese tunic clinging to her slender body, her face carefully made up to conceal her advanced age, a long ivory cigarette holder, and, especially effective, a faithful servant following at her heels.

For many years now, the Princess Li Chang has been showing up once a month at the "Gambling Hell" in Macao. The scenario is always the same. In the morning she boards the hydrofoil that regularly skims over the water from Hong Kong to Macao. During the crossing she installs herself on the deck, in order to get a better view of the small islands on the way, all the while inhaling the salt air. Her servant holds a Chinese parasol to protect her from the sun. The arrival at Macao is in high style. The servant goes first and helps his mistress across the gangplank. Then the princess proceeds in stately fashion toward her shrine, the Floating Casino (Illus. 169).

With the dignity of a "grande dame" she proceeds to the restaurant on the main floor, while her servant repairs to a canteen. Princess Li Chang then delicately nibbles on the specialties of the Floating Casino, while watching a Chinese opera being presented for the enjoyment of the restaurant's patrons. About two hours later, the princess goes upstairs to the game rooms. She casts an amused eye on the blackjack tables and then enters the private room reserved for poker players. Our princess is a loser and one would expect the Casino staff to be sympathetic to her. But this is not the case, for the princess has one fault. She doesn't like to lose. And yet she does lose every time. She becomes enraged, upsets an ashtray or jostles a croupier, and leaves, protesting that she is the injured party. Her servant is beside himself and can barely keep up with her on the way out. Once outside, she hails a taxi and returns to the boat landing.

The first time that I observed the princess behaving in this fashion, I became aware of the extraordinary trickery this lady practiced in order to help an accomplice win. It took an exceptional temperament to play to perfection the role of "The Angry Princess" in order to set in motion an incredible series of manipulations.

The strategy employed by the princess is as follows: the accomplice signals his hand to her through a visual code (the position of his hands in holding the cards). The princess then looks over her own hand to see if there is anything there that would be of use to her friend. If there is, she signals him to bet heavily and transmits in code the value of the cards she will provide him with. For example, the accomplice may have the Eight, Nine and Ten of Hearts, the Three of Spades and the King of Clubs. The princess has in her hand the Seven and Jack of Hearts, the Four of Clubs, the Eight of Diamonds and the Queen of Spades. All she has to do, therefore, is to give her accomplice the Seven and the Jack of Hearts for him to get a straight flush. And that's exactly what she does, right under everybody's nose. Her accomplice discreetly palms the two unwanted cards (Three of Spades and King of Clubs), placing them on his lap or under the table, while laying the three Hearts, piled one on top of the other as though there were still five cards. The princess has palmed in her right hand the two desirable cards (Seven and Jack of Hearts) while putting her other three cards on the table. She holds herself in readiness.

Another player raises the stakes against her accomplice. The

169 The floating Casino of Macao, one of the temples of the Gambling Hell.

princess throws in her hand and rests her elbow on her cards so that the attendant can't pick them up. She watches attentively. At the moment of calling, her accomplice declares a straight flush, but doesn't show it. The princess cries, "Oh no! That's too much!" and with a nervous movement secretly adds her two cards to those of her accomplice, turns them up and displays five cards. Plainly to be seen are the Seven, Jack, Eight, Nine and Ten of Hearts. She throws her three cards in the face of the accomplice, hurling abuse at him also. The cards land on the accomplice's lap. He picks them up, adding the two unwanted cards that he had palmed earlier, and immediately gives these five cards to the croupier. The princess leaves. The victim pays up. The accomplice complains about the attitude of the princess, but pockets his winnings and calmly goes on playing.

117

I left the room shortly after Li Chang and followed her discreetly. I got aboard the same hydrofoil and watched her during the crossing. She had the pleased look of a child that had pulled off a successful prank. I was eager to talk to her, but did not know how to go about it. On arriving in Hong Kong, I made up my mind. I overtook her on the pier, presented my card to her and invited her to dinner. The princess recoiled before this bold behavior, looked me full in the face, glanced around as though to see whether I was alone, and to the amazement of her servant, accepted my invitation.

Yielding to the princess's wishes we went to the skyview restaurant on top of the Hotel Hilton. For about half an hour we talked only about the menu, while admiring Hong Kong Bay, covered with junks shimmering against the background of the buildings of Kowloon Peninsula. Then I started talking about my profession, my research project and my admiration for her superior technique. Without overdoing it, I worked into the conversation what I had discovered in Macao and also the pleasure I took in having dinner with her. The princess turned out to be a marvelous source of travel information, telling me about everything that I could still discover in the area. Then, somewhat suspicious of my request, she gave me permission to describe her system in my book, provided, however, that I waited six months. That was over a year ago. I have no hesitation (in revealing her method) because I have heard from a friend in Macao that the princess has disappeared. Has she gone into retirement or is she having her "fits of anger" in some other poker room? I hope to find out some day.

8. The Secret Powers of the Card Sharps

The true professionals among card sharps subject themselves to an intensive training régime, some of whose aspects have been kept top secret until now.

170 **The Master Cheat has superhuman capacities thanks to special disciplines.**

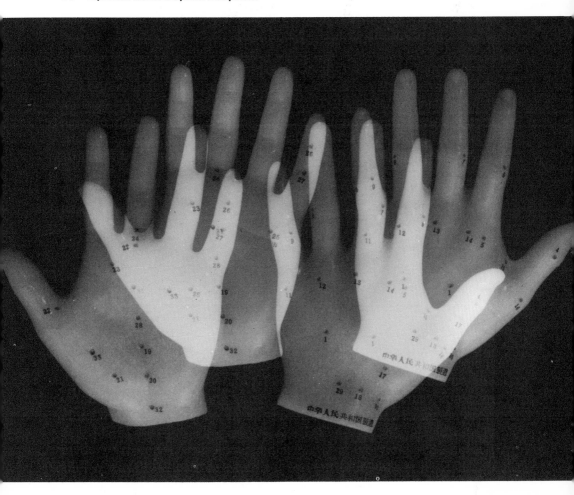

The Fingers Acquire Autonomy

Limbering up exercises

Rigidity of the carpus (wrist bone), metacarpus (bones of the hand) and phalanges (finger bones) can be overcome by manipulations that are on the order of massaging, kneading and stretching. These manipulations should be done in the order shown below.

1. Close your fists (Illus. 171) and open them abruptly, stretching your fingers wide (Illus. 172). Do this 20 times in succession first. Then gradually increase the number of times until you can do it 50 times.

171

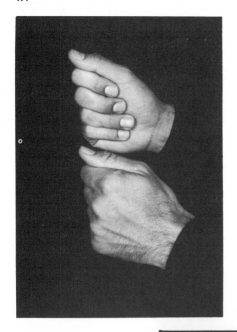

172

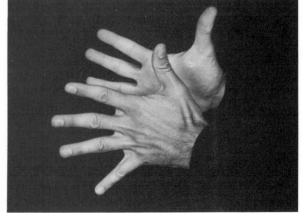

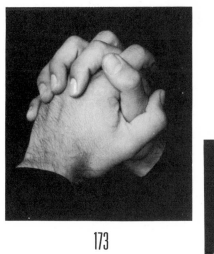

173

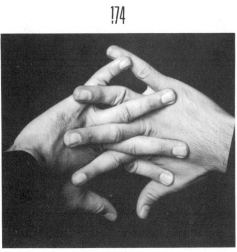

174

2. Clasp your hands (Illus. 173) and bend them back as you draw them apart (Illus. 174). Do this about 5 times in succession.

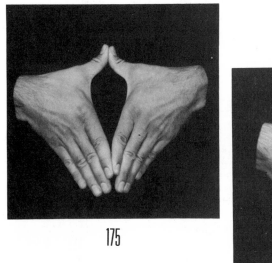

175

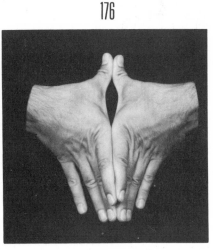

176

3. Hold your hands in the position shown (Illus. 175) and push them together gently (Illus. 176). Do this three times in succession.

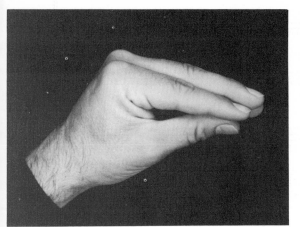
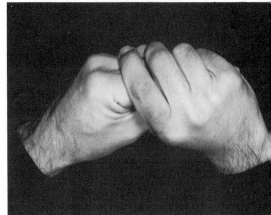

177 178

4. Place the fingers of the left hand in the position shown (Illus. 177). Enclose the fingers in your right hand and turn your hands outward, squeezing gently (Illus. 178). Reverse the role of the hands. Do this 5 times for each hand.

5. Wiggle the fingers of both hands wildly and rapidly (Illus. 179) for about 30 seconds.

Exercise for the muscles of the little finger

Thanks to the appropriate kinesitherapy (treatment by means of exercise) you can develop the muscles of your hypothenar (the mound at the base of the little finger) in a way that will help palm a card more easily. A simple way to develop it is to hang a key ring on the little finger (Illus. 180) and raise it 20 or 30 times in succession. You should add a key every two weeks but don't exercise with more than 10 keys of average weight on the ring at one time.

179

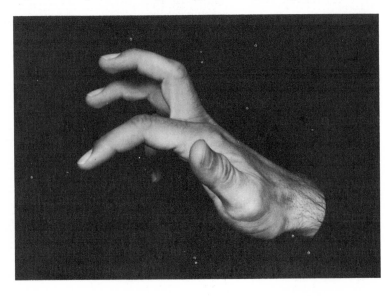

180

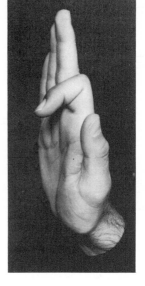

181

Exercises in self-mastery

Anatomically, the thumb has flexor and extensor tendons of its own which give an independent movement, while the four fingers are virtually served by a common system of tendons. The card sharp thus is obliged to make a superhuman effort to train these fingers in a special way that will enable them to develop independence of movement.

1. Bend each finger without bending any of the others at the same time (Illus. 181, 182, 183, 184).

182

183

184

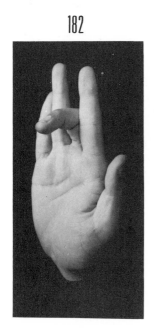
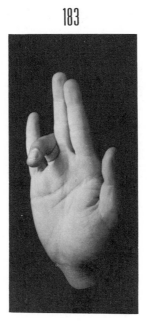
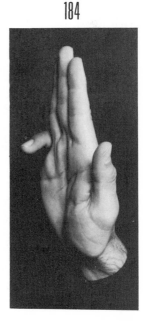

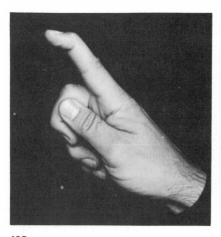

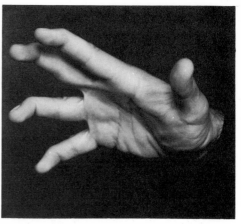

185

186

187

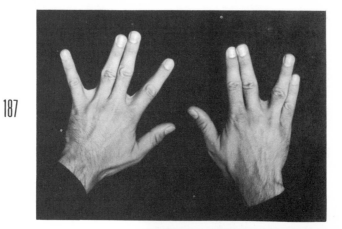

188

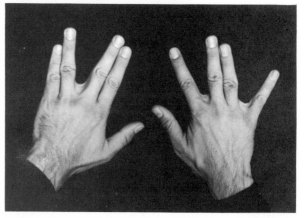

2. Bend the tip of the index finger without bending the middle joint (Illus. 185). Do the same for all 4 fingers at once (Illus. 186).

3. Spread your fingers differently for each hand, as in Illus. 187. Reverse the positions of the right and left hands in a single movement (Illus. 188).

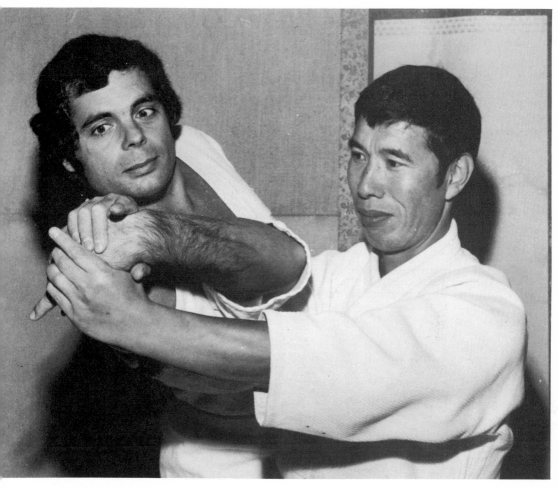

Aiki-Do and suppleness of the wrist.
Total harmony resides in Master Noro
(right), the teacher.

The Body Stays in Harmony

Regular workouts in classic gymnastics are indispensable if you wish to maintain physical equilibrium, but certain forms of athletics are better suited to the needs of the card sharps than others.

Thus Aiki-Do, a Japanese discipline, develops wrist suppleness enormously without isolating the wrist from the rest of the body, but rather maintaining an overall harmony (Illus. 189).

Exercises inducing relaxation and meditation are presented by the instructor to develop the inner peace of Zen, a state most useful to the card sharp when plying his trade. Mentally, he must become the man who is running the game, at the same time keeping up his smile and maintaining control over his muscles.

Baton exercises. The precision of the movements is patiently demonstrated by Professor Jean Lafont.

Workouts with a baton (Illus. 190) aid other wrist movements and develop elegance of gesture.

Obviously, yoga is ideal for relaxing the card sharp before a game. Especially the exercises where the legs are held up in the air, causing blood to rush to the head, and also the lotus position. Finish this off with a period of total relaxation and a few breathing exercises.

We also advise card sharps of mediocre ability to develop their running speed, which they will find very useful if they are unmasked.

The Successful Régime

It's practically an ascetic life. The card sharp should abstain from anything stimulating, such as coffee or tea, in order to maintain his self-control. On the other hand he can gorge on sweets, since glucose promotes oxygenation in the brain cells. Above all, no clear spirits. In a pinch, whisky is an excellent vasodilator, augmenting the circulation of the blood in the heart and brain. Fruit juices are recommended for they contain ascorbic acid (vitamin C) which has an oxygen-reducing effect on the general metabolism. The latest American discoveries in this field indicate that foods containing thyramine should be avoided as it is a frequent cause of migraine and disturbances of the central nervous system. Things especially to be avoided are chocolate, cheese, yogurt and red wine.

In any case, meals should be on the light side, for the negative effect of slow digestion on the mental processes is well known. Sexual activity should be limited, and in no case should it take place less than $3\frac{1}{2}$ hours before cheating at cards, for it dangerously disturbs the mental processes. Some card sharps recommend a cold shower on getting up, accompanied by a rubdown with a friction glove. Others stress the need to pay attention to the functioning of the intestines. A maximum of sleep is also required—at least seven hours, in any case.

Golden Needles

Acupuncture is used by very few physicians in the West, as opposed to the Far East. It allows the card sharp to treat himself. In fact, if he keeps a few needles in his pocket, he can shut himself up in the toilet (before the game) and give himself a fast treatment. It's enough for him to do it on the ears or hands for about five minutes.

Ear therapy

The ear does not respond to the classic laws of yin and yang. Therefore to gain the desired end, steel needles are the perfect method. The less often one uses the needles, it should be pointed out, the more beneficial and durable the effects.

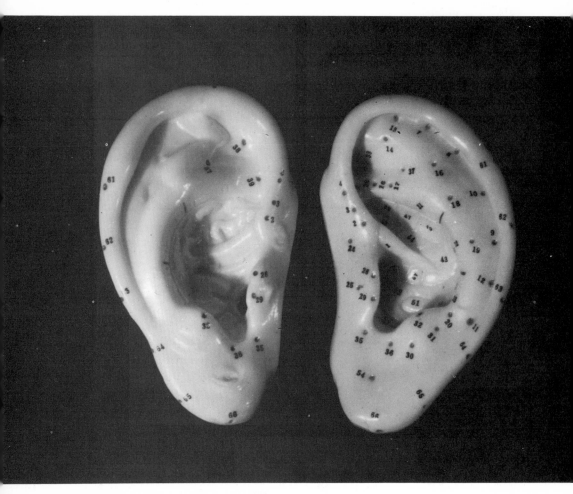

Ear therapy: ordinary steel needles
stuck into certain spots increase the
mastery of the card sharp.

The most effective spots for acupuncture (on the ear) are 14,
which affects the fingers; 23, which counteracts nervous twitching;
31, which greatly benefits the eyes; and 42, which facilitates total
relaxation (Illus. 191).

Acupuncture on the hands

We shall only mention two places where needles are inserted.
4, for the eyesight; 16 to increase mental perception (Illus. 192).

Psychotronics

This term was used officially in 1967 in Prague by Dr. Zdenek Reydak. It concerns the study of phenomena in which energy is released by the process of thinking or by the propulsion of human will power. This energy may be as capable of transferring information as it is of engendering physical action. The concept "psychotronics" touches upon that of "parapsychology," which is in the field of psychology, and also upon "metapsychology," which is more in the realm of physiology. Their common object of study lies in three major series of phenomena: paranormal information or "clairvoyance," paranormal communication or "telepathy," and paranormal acts or "psychokinesis." These phenomena seem susceptible of partially throwing off the usual limitations of time, space and motion.

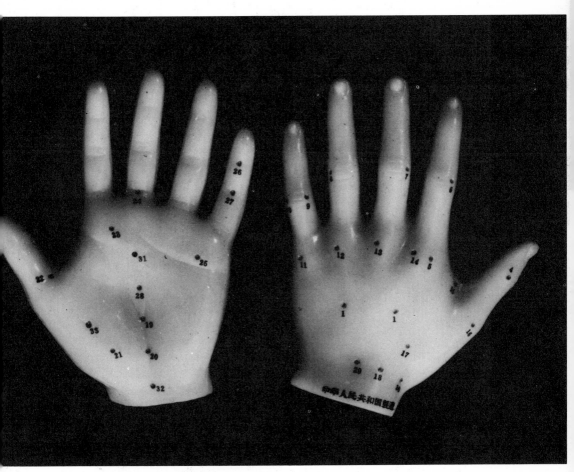

192 Acupuncture on the hands: the work of gold needles prepares the card sharp perfectly for his work.

Modern experiments in these fields are being carried out in laboratories according to scientific method. The experiments are completely automated and use animals as subjects, thereby minimizing the chances of fraud. The results are incontestably conclusive. The increased use of contingency methods shows that man, animals and living matter in general can affect any unstable physical phenomenon and can often adapt it to their needs.

Many card sharps are aware of these studies and are seeking to apply them to the outcome of gambling. Numerous specialists have told me that they owe their success only to these phenomena. Clairvoyance enables them to know what the card on top of the pack is, or at least to come pretty close to it. Obviously, it is telepathy that gets the most results. But this requires a transmitting agent who is in tune with the card sharp. A sudden change of players can jeopardize everything. For this reason this kind of trickster (telepathic) prefers to play with friends, contenting himself with small winnings. Often he does it solely for the fun of it.

What I have found most satisfying in this field is the application of psychokinesis. Indeed, I have met a poker player who concentrated strongly on a certain hand before the cards were dealt. Another player shuffled and dealt. Through a psychotronic effect, the desired hand was dealt to the trickster. This man assured me that he could do this only once in the course of an evening, having practiced yoga exercises for an hour before playing. How many lucky players apply this principle without knowing it, simply by means of their desire to win?

9. Truth Serum

A "born" card sharp is much more a great psychologist than an adroit manipulator.

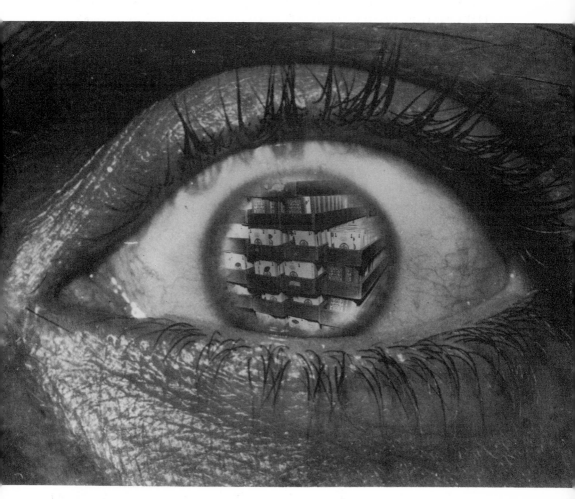

193 The card sharp sees the world in terms of playing cards.

Psychology or Experience?

General attitude: The professional card sharp, of course, has a cover-up profession that allows him to display a certain amount of wealth. He doesn't seem interested in money and if he places a bet, it is, he says, only to heighten the interest of the game. He places a small bet at the beginning. He shows a great deal of trust and readily hands over a wallet full of money or important papers, for safekeeping. Clearly, he is a psychologist, but he doesn't show it. He even seems somewhat stupid. He's a nice guy, but something is missing. He complains about various illnesses or physical weaknesses. Above all, he seems awkward, holds his cards badly—not too much so, just a little. The card sharp possesses above all a quality without which all others would be useless. He recognizes opportunity.

The Science of Distracting Attention

The card sharp often pretends to have poor eyesight, which gives him the opportunity to drop something when he wants to switch packs, for example. There must be a reason for any abnormal movement required by his trickery—it must look natural to the other players. Thus, he flicks away a bit of cigarette ash with a card before shuffling, which gives him a chance to crimp the card against the table.

Starting to sneeze causes a movement of the right hand toward the nose, while the left hand changes the cut.

The Card Sharp's Team

Except in very rare cases, the true professional card sharp doesn't work alone. All their coups are the result of teamwork and they work out an actual strategy. The "decoy" is responsible for finding a sucker, or simply pointing one out. He is a player, also. He applies his skills to get the sucker desirous of playing with his friend, a friend he'll vouch for. Of course, the "decoy" has to lose, so that the sucker won't get suspicious; and he has to show by his resignation and even temper that he has the right philosophy for a loser.

International card sharps travel endlessly. They exchange names of "decoys" that have previously worked with them.

The "switcher" is responsible for putting stacked packs in the place of those to be used in a game. To do this he must resort to actual burglary sometimes, but most of the time it's enough to draw off the person in charge of the drawer or cabinet where the cards are kept. A simple method, and one often used, consists of buying 10 blue packs at a shop regularly patronized by honest players who prefer blue packs.

When hardly out of the door, the switcher goes back into the shop and says that on second thought he prefers red cards. The vendor sees no inconvenience in exchanging them, most of the time. The card sharp then hands him 10 other packs that have been previously marked. Thus there is a strong chance that the honest players buying these packs before the game will buy marked decks without the vendor's knowing it.

Some card sharps employ a prostitute whose duty it is to tire out the sucker before the game. It is thanks to this system that numerous unlucky players have had a chance to verify the proverb, "lucky in love, but unlucky at cards."

The history of trickery shows that employees of casinos, clubs, shops and factories have sometimes been the accomplices of a card sharp.

It is for this reason that these establishments are very exacting in recruiting personnel.

The sucker often doesn't have enough money to pay the card sharp immediately, and arranges to settle the debt in a day or two. This is a classic gambling debt. But from time to time, a sucker will have suspicions, change his mind and refuse to pay. The card sharp then appeals to a collector. This is generally a man of good family, having good manners and an imposing aspect. His probity and his connections are without question. He earns 10 per cent of the amount of the debt. Most of the time this person is extremely upright and does not concern himself with whether the winner has cheated or not. His lofty aim is above all to see that promises are respected.

Psychoanalysis of the Card Sharp

Except for the card sharp who learned his trade in his own family circle—secrets and tricks of the trade passed on from one generation to another, or from friend to friend—card sharps are usually veritable pathological cases.

The card sharp is a paranoiac with masochistic tendencies. In effect, he may have experienced a considerable frustration in childhood, traces of which can still be found under analysis, and this engendered an immense desire to dominate. He wants to be sure to win, so he cheats. Behind his sociable appearance, the cheat feels a genuine hatred for society. He is very much alone. The act of cheating, of course, triggers a certain anguish in conjunction with the stimulus of domination. This anxiety becomes very exciting. The greater the risk, the greater the card sharp's pleasure. The disequilibrium nonetheless can become so great that cheating no longer satisfies the desire for "fear." This is why many great card sharps have gone on to play roulette, at which they cannot cheat. At this point, the anguish is total. The sense of loss also.

This masochistic process has also been experienced by numerous players who did not cheat. The history of England reveals to us that one day George III asked Charles James Fox what in his opinion was the greatest pleasure that could be felt. "To win at gambling," replied the statesman. "And after that pleasure, what?" asked the King. "Losing at gambling," replied Fox.

The honest player, when he has lost everything, is often better off than if he had money to gamble, for he knows that he must go back to leading a normal life and doesn't have to engage in the pathological behavior of shutting himself up in a gaming room.

That makes us think of the addict drawn back to his source of supply when he has money. From this point of view, the card sharp is for the card player what a psychiatrist is for a drug addict. It is an understandable evil, if not a necessary one.

10. The Cheat and the Law

194 The Director of the Sporting de Monte-Carlo is a specialist in organized gambling. His job is to protect players to the maximum from possible cheaters.

The Casino Watchers

The directors of the casino of Monte Carlo, with the agreement of the representatives of their employees' trade union, have divulged for the first time all the details of their surveillance system. At different stages, the card sharp finds himself faced with practically insurmountable difficulties. The ingenious arrangements installed by the casino are the result of many years' experience and have been created in response to different kinds of trickery. Every casino in Europe (except for France) and the United States has total liberty to protect itself against possible cheats and also maintains its own security guards. In France, the method is different, for the casinos are under the Ministry of the Interior, and if they have any doubts about a player, they are supposed to call the police gambling squad. The system in use in Monte Carlo has been adopted by other non-French casinos and liaison is maintained by the gambling inspector in their respective countries.

The Employees of the Monte Carlo Casino

I was received very kindly by the Director General, M. Pascal-Albert Biancheri, who was willing to answer all my questions. The managing committee clearly controls all the various operations of the casino. M. Biancheri has a sizable surveillance team at his disposal, reporting directly to the Deputy Director. Each gaming room has two surveillance men, and naturally the croupiers and other staff members also observe the players, and are specially trained to detect any unusual movement. Beyond this, an inspector is responsible for the room. The "physiognomist," as his name indicates, has the job of refusing admission to anyone he recognizes as a card sharp. The television crew makes up the newest unit watching for possible cheats. But above all, the employees are truly hand-picked and clearly have a great integrity.

The Travels of a Pack of Cards

Every morning, the man in charge of the cards (the *cartier*) comes to get new packs of cards. The number of packs he needs is taken from a special locker. The packs are numbered. The attendant must sign a register giving his name, the time, the date and number of packs taken. He then brings the packs of cards to the tables. Each croupier displays the packs and even counts them in front of the players, if it is *chemin de fer* or baccarat. But even for *chemin de fer* the cards may be counted on the demand of a player. If a patron

195 The television surveillance room at Monte Carlo. Each screen can magnify the hand of a player suspected of cheating.

asks to shuffle the cards, he is allowed to do so, but the croupier will still give them a final shuffle.

At the end of the game, the cards are counted again and verified by the *cartier*, who can then catch any anomalies—marks, crimps, missing cards, for example. Then the *cartier* takes the packs back to the locker, signing the register once again. One employee is especially responsible for destroying the cards that have been used.

Closed-circuit Television

Several television cameras are cleverly embodied in the décor and make it possible to observe any players making unusual movements. These highly-developed cameras can zoom in on a hand or a card and blow it up sufficiently so that the honesty of the player can be checked out and it can be determined whether he may be a threat to the other players. In a special room, two observers scrutinize the

196 From his office, M. Biancheri can watch any room in the Monte Carlo casino that he wants to.

screens and receive and pass on instructions by telephone (Illus. 195).

As a last resort, the Director General has a set in his office that can get any channel (Illus. 196). M. Biancheri assures us, in addition, "This equipment is the perfect means of guaranteeing the honesty of the game and thus protecting the interests of the players. The only people that need to be afraid of this surveillance system are potential cheats."

Transformation of a Shoe

Improvements in a device used by the Casino often come about as a result of attempts at cheating. M. Biancheri told me the story of a card-dispensing shoe that was transformed right after a dishonest player was caught in the act. This man managed to palm several cards by moving close to the upper opening of the shoe when his turn came, while drawing a card from the bottom with his thumb in the normal fashion. This act of palming was really quite a feat of virtuosity. The cheat then secretly passed the palmed cards to an accomplice. The accomplice then went off unobtrusively to the lavatory, and arranged the cards in a certain order. He came back to the table and handed the cards to the cheat who managed to return the cards to the shoe, effecting the same manoeuvre, but in reverse. He was thus assured of several coups. His extraordinary stratagem was discovered, nonetheless. The management promptly installed small bars on the opening to prevent any further attempts of this sort. Eventually, the tops of shoes were sealed hermetically at the time of their manufacture.

Manufacturers' Guarantee

All the details on manufacturing playing cards for use in casinos were given to us by M. Jean-Marie Simon, who directs one of the main European card factories at Nancy, France.

197 In his card factory, M. Simon checks the working of the automatic production line.

Manufacture of Cards

1. Special cardboard is furnished by a factory in Germany which guarantees that there are no impurities or imperfections that could serve as marks on the backs of cards.

2. The plates of cards are printed by the offset process.

3. The prints are then passed over rollers which coat them with a mixture of varnish and stearate to make them slippery.

4. They are next run across another set of rollers to "iron" them at 120°C. (250°F). As they come off the rollers, they are rehumidified.

5. The prints are next cut up by special machines and assembled into packs.

6. The packs are then wrapped in cellophane.

7. The last three operations, formerly done by hand, are now performed by an automatic assembly-line method that is absolutely remarkable (Illus. 197).

Inspection of Cards for Casinos

This inspection is carried out in a special room with the aid of special equipment. It is done by a team of hand-picked employees.

198 Cards for casinos are carefully sorted. The least defect causes them to be eliminated.

A checker makes sure that each pack is complete by superimposing a transparent panel.

1. One worker first examines all the cards systematically and pulls out any that have a defect, however minute (Illus. 198). This precaution results in the discarding of about 35 per cent of the cards, a huge proportion.

2. A second worker checks to see that a pack is complete, using a special board on which she lines up all the cards. Then she lowers a transparent panel on which all the cards in the pack are depicted, superimposing it on the cards. She can then see whether the pack is complete (Illus. 199).

3. A third employee wraps the cards by hand in special cellophane sealed at 5 different spots by a special cement, in such a way that anyone who tries to tamper with the pack will be obliged to break the wrapping (Illus. 200). And even then, some years back some card sharps succeeded in opening this wrapping delicately, cutting it in a certain way so that they could reseal it after, naturally, they had doctored the cards by crimping some of them so that they could spot them later. The police investigated the factory, but M. Simon was able to prove easily that the doctoring of the cards had been done outside, after they had been sold. He did this by showing that the cellophane wrapping was 5 mm shorter than the wrapping of a normal pack.

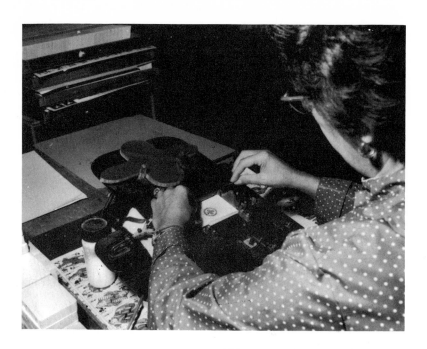

4. A fourth worker puts a set of six packs into a cardboard box, closes it, seals it and numbers it. When these boxes are sent to the casinos, they are accompanied by a list of these numbers, in response to a purchase order issued by the casino and approved by the police.

M. Jean-Marie Simon also declared, "My profession of master card manufacturer obliges me to take constant pains to furnish a product that meets the specifications of the players and guarantees them the maximum security against possible trickery."

Due to preventive police work, the field of action for the card sharp has become so narrow that any act of cheating tends to fall within the scope of abnormal behavior, especially since the shoe has come into use and the cards have been transformed. The letters and numbers in the corners of the cards have disappeared, the size of the cards has been increased from 5.5 x 8.5 cm to 6.75 x 9.75 cm, making it practically impossible to manipulate them fraudulently (Illus. 201). Furthermore, a veritable ritual of do's and don'ts has been set up. The patrons of casinos and clubs have realized these minutely detailed regulations, far from being a nuisance, provide an additional guarantee of honest gambling.

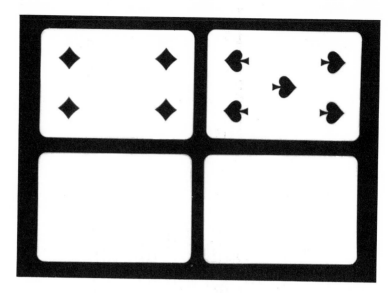

201 The casino cards have no letters or numbers in the corner and the back is plain. Furthermore their large size prevents virtually all palming.

11. The Card Sharps of the Year 2000

202 Techniques of the future will give the card sharp victories without problems.

New Gadgets

The card sharps of the future will have extraordinary technical means at their disposal. It will be very difficult for honest players to be sure that their partners are not cheating. Honest playing will only be assured by electronic and chemical methods. This technical warfare will be similar to what already is going on in espionage. But, in fact, have not some sophisticated cheats already acquired mastery over these methods?

The Euphoria-Inducing Cigar

This cigar contains an electronic system that opens a capsule of compressed gas (Illus. 203). All that needs to be done is to bite gently on the cigar to start the contact. The gas used is a derivative of nitrogen protoxide (which in heavy concentration is used in anaesthesia). The application is very effective. Just before making a big coup, the ejection of a few whiffs of gas will make the other players careless. In a few minutes they will be so relaxed that they will play with total confidence, and no suspicions. A simple antidote pill taken an hour earlier by the card sharp gives him immunity from the gas.

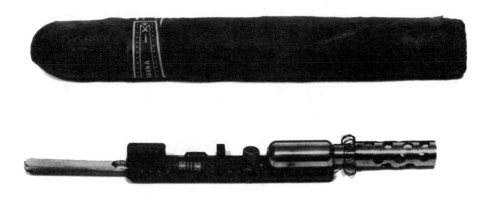

203 Euphoria-inducing cigar. Ideal for allaying the suspicions of other players.

The Relaxation Reservoir

This little tank is very practical (Illus. 204). It has a small opening that discharges a liquid (A); a clasp intended to be attached to a ring worn by the card sharp (B); and a little pouch made of flexible plastic (C). The liquid used is a derivative of mono-amino-oxydase (used in medicine as the "happiness pill").

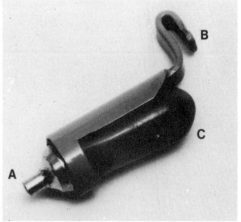

204 The tranquillity reservoir. Perfect for making the suckers happy even when they've lost everything.

The application of this calls for a little practice. The cheat has to arrange to pass a glass of whisky to the player that he wants to "neutralize." This can be accomplished during a break, and well in advance of the critical point in the game. The little reservoir has to be pressed against the rim of the glass (Illus. 205). The liquid drops into the drink of the victim, who will start "soaring" after he takes a drink, and he will no longer be a problem for the cheat.

205 How the reservoir is used undetected.

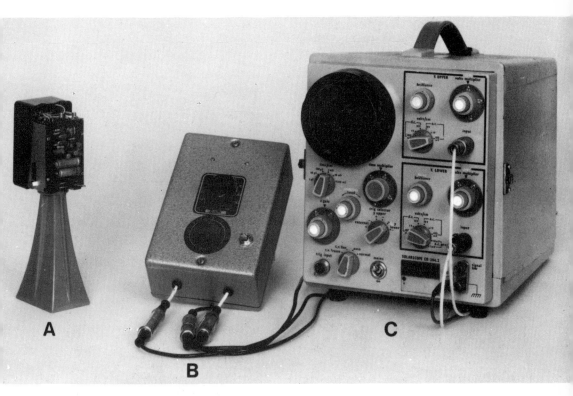

206 Radar (A) with radioactive particles, containing a transmitter (B) and an electronic oscilloscope (C).

Radioactive Particles

Playing cards are marked invisibly. They have been impregnated with a combination of radioactive elements. Cerium 144-Iodine 131 (140 KEV). The proportion of the radioactive elements varies from one card to another in a way that can be identified electronically. The methods of scanning and transmitting vary, according to the place where the cheating is going on.

Hyper-Frequency Radar

If the cheat is going to operate away from home, this method is the best. The radar apparatus (Illus. 206-A) is placed in a small suitcase hidden in a room located above the one where the game

147

will be held. The hyper-frequency radar operates in the 10 GEGA HERTS band. The length of the wave makes it possible to travel through walls and detect radioactive particles with a GUMM diode and a STOKY. This apparatus also includes a decoder-transmitter that sends information to the card sharp. This is done in clear wording through sound signals picked up in a receiver attached to the card sharp's ear, or by means of a binary system in the case of a tactile receiver.

From a nearby building or even in a small truck, accomplices can check out the game thanks to a receiver (Illus. 206-B) attached to an oscilloscope (Illus. 206-C) indicating visually the cards of each player. The transmission of information on each card is very rapid, but the trained operators can read it without trouble. The "writing" is naturally special, as seen in the example of the Two of Diamonds (Illus. 207).

207 Appearance of the Two of Diamonds on the screen.

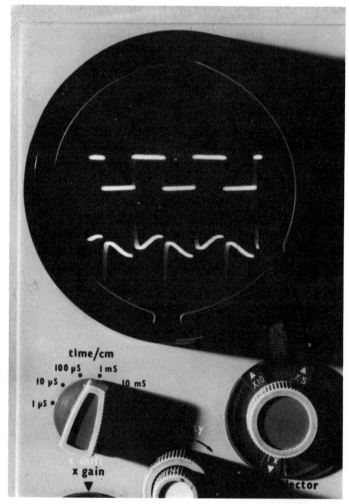

The man checking the oscilloscope can thus determine whether to have an accomplice end the game or simply slow it up, according to necessity.

208 Clairvoyance crystal. A veritable crystal ball that never makes a mistake.

The Crystal of Clairvoyance

When the card sharp plays in his own home, the table can have at the place of each player a Tholium INA crystal collimated for a precise zone (Illus. 208). Each crystal is connected to a photomultiplier. All are tied into a transmitter or are joined up with a computer in the next room (for example a Multi-8 Intertechnical). The latter is programmed to indicate the cards of each player. The operator can speak in a normal voice into a micro-transmitter, and be heard by the card sharp at the table, who has a receiver connected to his ear.

Intra-Cranial Receivers

A player suspected of cheating can always be subjected to a systematic search. Therefore it is in the interest of card cheats to undergo a surgical operation, in which a miniaturized receiver is lodged inside their skulls. A specialist surgeon told me the details, without telling me, however, what the fees are for such an operation, one that surely doesn't yet come under the scope of Social Security.

Pre-operative assessment of patient's condition

After the precautionary examination undertaken before any surgery, radiographs and tomograms are made of the middle ear and inner ear in order to determine the most suitable place to

209 Intra-cranial receiver with its electronic components and printed circuit.

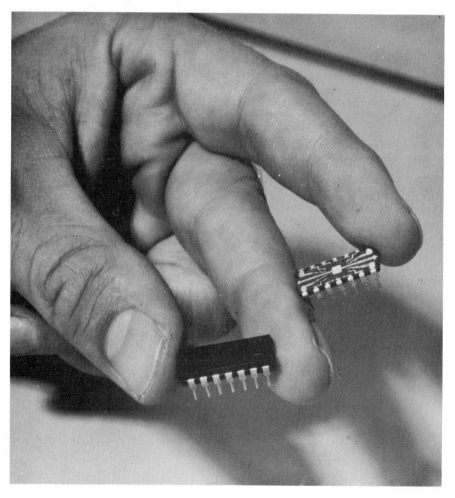

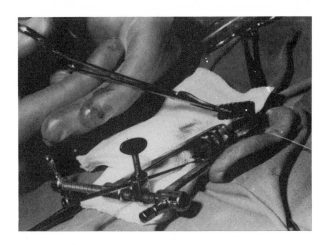

210 Surgical operation: starting to put the receiver in place.

install the receiver. This operation cannot be done on those who have diabetes, cancer, tuberculosis, blood diseases and diseases affecting coagulation of the blood. Chronic otitis (inflammation of the ear) and auricular suppuration (discharge of pus in the ear) also rule out this operation.

The receptor is previously sterilized for 10 days in formaldehyde vapor, along with its electronic components and circuits (Illus. 209).

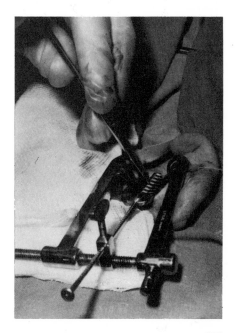

211 Final positioning of receiver in the outer surface of the mastoid.

Operation

The patient is anaesthetized with penthoral-curare-oxygen by tracheal intubation. The surgeon makes an incision above and behind the ear, which enables him to loosen the outer ear and bend it down, thanks to an orthostatic receiver (Illus. 210). The surgeon then trepans the outer surface of the mastoid with an electric drill, to make a niche having the exact dimensions of the intra-cranial device. The device is then put in place (Illus. 211). It is tested to see if it works. The ear is then sutured in its original position with a very fine nylon thread, that in a month will leave a totally invisible scar.

Charging batteries

As with a pacemaker, which is a much more common device used in heart surgery, it is necessary to charge the batteries every two years. A local anaesthetic and a minimal incision are enough. There's even no need for hospitalization.

12. Your Turn to Play

—If you think that taxes are too light and you would like to supplement them, while having fun at the same time:
PLAY IN CASINOS OR GAMBLING CLUBS.

—If you want to win money and avoid paying taxes on it, and especially if you are not afraid of losing (for some time or other a professional or amateur cheat will fleece you):
GET INTO PRIVATE GAMES.

—If you want to impoverish your family or be driven to suicide through despair and ruination:
BET HEAVILY.

—If you are unemployed and fed up:
PLAY WITHOUT THINKING.

—If you dream of being knifed on a street corner, or of ending your days peacefully in prison:
CHEAT.

—But if you want to practice card manipulations for fun and stay honest:
DO AS I DO . . .

And in any case: Good Luck,

Gerard Majax

Index